Be
"The Other Woman"
in Your Man's Life

Be
"The Other Woman"
in Your Man's Life

KAREN HOLDER

iUniverse, Inc.
Bloomington

Be "The Other Woman" in Your Man's Life

iUniverse books may be ordered through booksellers or by contacting:

iUniverse
1663 Liberty Drive
Bloomington, IN 47403
www.iuniverse.com
1-800-Authors (1-800-288-4677)

ISBN: 978-1-4759-4507-2 (sc)
ISBN: 978-1-4759-4508-9 (ebk)

Library of Congress Control Number: 2012916126

Printed in the United States of America

iUniverse rev. date: 10/25/2012

To my husband Bobby,
"My Prince Charming"
You make all my little girl dreams come true.
Thank you for your love and support during my journey.
I know at times it was not easy!

To my "Beautiful" daughter Kimberly,
You are one of the most precious gifts
Ever given to me. I love you so much.

To my son Brian,
I see the sun rising and
The moon shining every time I see you smile.
"I Hope You Dance"

Contents

Acknowledgements

To my sweet friend Rebecca,
I will always be grateful for your friendship and
the help you gave me getting my manuscript started.

To my final editor and wonderful crazy friend Brenda Blackwelder,
Thank you for your guidance, the extra typing and encouraging me
all the times I just wanted to throw my computer out the window!

To the editorial team at IUniverse,
Krista and Mars, thank you for your support
In turning my dream into reality.

Last but certainly not least,
I want to give a "special" thank you for those customers who
gave me the inspiration to write this book.
If I have helped just one woman,
then all my efforts and sleepless nights have been worthwhile.

Introduction

I decided to write this book in honor of my customers and all the stories they have shared with me, both good and bad. Some of the stories were painful, from women who were cheated on or taken advantage of in other ways. Some stories came from women who were so uninhibited that they gave me too much information, which I found a little scary at times.

But some of the hardest information I obtained for this book came from men, the ones who hit on me. Some were married; some were not. But even though all of them knew I was happily married, they still tried to woo me. Some, sadly enough, were just looking for a little attention, while some longtime customers, where I knew both wife and husband, wanted me to talk their wives into wearing more sexy clothing, both in and out of the bedroom.

When I opened my lingerie boutique in 1986 on the grounds of Wake Forest University in Winston-Salem, I thought my small, picturesque boutique would fulfill all my dreams. I had recently married my handsome and charming second husband, who taught me how to snow ski as well as climb mountains. We even bathed naked in a cool mountain stream on a glorious day, something I had never ever considered. Even though these adventures brought excitement to a sometimes boring week of work and life's problems, I thought I had married the man with whom I would live happily ever after. However, life had its way with me.

I became a flight attendant, and to make a long story short, I found myself realizing that I just was not fulfilled. (I also observed a lot while I was a flight attendant. Believe me, I could write another book on what I learned and saw on my overnight trips.)

The second husband and I were at a crossroads in our marriage, and I felt I needed something more. I knew I loved him, but we just seemed to want different things in life. One day while working a flight, I accidentally ran into the man I had dated ten years before marrying the second husband and realized that the love I had felt for him had not died. He was still single. Did fate have him waiting for me? We married in 1991, and that is another story.

I believe everyone truly does have a soul mate, and when you finally find yours, you should do everything in your power to keep that special thing that brought you together alive and new forever. I believe that no one enters marriage with the intention of getting divorced. We all think we will be the perfect couple, the one to beat the odds. Ours, we think, will be the fairy tale wedding with a "happily ever after" ending, like Cinderella and Prince Charming. Then one day, we wake up and wonder, "What the hell happened?" It is called "life" with all its ups and downs.

I personally feel that marriage is always a challenge. It's like the fragile orchid, needing constant care and attention to live. You have to really love the orchid for it to survive, and now I know that we need to forever treat our partner as if we are still dating, with the same attentiveness we give to our beloved orchid.

That is what *Be the Other Woman in Your Man's Life* is all about. It is about tending to the commitment, communication, compassion, and, most importantly, passion in your relationship to keep it alive and thriving. It is about taking our vows seriously, like our grandparents and our great-grandparents did. Sometimes we don't accept our own frailties; we forget our commitment to stay together forever through thick and thin. In today's world, it seems that, with the divorce rate so high, we dispose of our marriages as easily as we do dirty diapers.

Also included are some of my personal experiences and the things I have learned in my past two failed marriages, the mistakes I made as well as learning what I need and want from my current marriage. My third (and final) marriage has had its ups and downs, but I believe we have created a duet, and we both love the music we now share. We will soon celebrate twenty years together.

But don't get me wrong. Life and the economy have put us down some rough and bumpy roads, but we just keep holding on to the steering wheel, even when we hit a dead-end road or suffer from the proverbial flat tire. I have made a lot of mistakes in my life, and I am very sorry for some, some I am not very proud of, but I have owned up to them and the demons that were in me. I used the knowledge to help me write this book in hopes it will help every woman who reads it.

Just remember, there really is such a thing as the "other woman." I did not make up that term. You can keep her at bay or let her into your life. It certainly is your choice. I hope you will decide to be the "other woman in your man's life."

I also would like to say I turned sixty this year, so:

I really feel
I have *been* there
did it
and have *done* it!
I totally *understand*
and I *get* it!

I know what it is like to speak to your husband and not be heard. My first husband of thirteen years, the father of my two beautiful children, never heard me. I used to say he would rather lie under the '55 Chevy he was rebuilding than lie under me!

I also know what it is like to give all you have to give to your children and feel you still have not done enough. Maybe I will forever feel that I will never do enough to make up for putting my children through a divorced home. I constantly wish I could have been strong enough to wait until they were of age.

There is always the feeling that you should have or could have done more. That compels you to go out and find just one more "perfect" gift for them on special days, hoping it will be enough to make up for putting them in a divorced family. It is the martyr in us.

I know what it is like to work two jobs and still not have enough money for just you. All I am trying to say is that, if you want to live happily ever after with your "Prince Charming," then you constantly have to work at it. You have to be a duet and love the same music forever.

While reading this book, I want you never to feel like I am putting women down. It is not my intention. I just want for us women to take charge. My father-in-law used to say, "Only one can be in charge at a time." So, with that excellent advice, be in charge! Take charge of your own destiny, and then teach it forward. You can have that fairy tale marriage ever after . . . or not.

What do you have to lose by trying my tried-and-true methods at least once a month . . . if not once a week? It can't hurt, and it could be a lot of fun!

If your marriage or relationship is showing signs of flickering out, you can do things to ignite the intimacy and put the romance back into your relationship. This book will show you how other women have used the techniques and tips to reestablish the love connection they shared with their partner when they first started dating. I hope this book will be able to improve your relationship without the expense of counselors.

Statistics show that happily married couples live longer, healthier lives than single people do. I believe that, if you nurture your relationship, love grows deeper with each year you are together. I believe in the institution of marriage, and I believe I finally married my Prince Charming! This book may offend some, but my great-grandmother used to say, "You can't please everyone." I only hope that I do please the majority of women. The women I write about are different from one another in many ways. Some are African American; others are Asian. Some are homosexual; others are heterosexual. Some are married; some are divorced. Some are single; some are separated. Some are older; others are younger. No matter what our differences, we have much in common. I personally pride myself in being open-minded and believe it has helped me learn a lot by not discriminating, thus enabling me to include much more information in this book.

Think about this. Why is the Statue of Liberty portrayed as a woman and not a man? Liberty is the right and power to act, believe, or express oneself in a manner of one's own choosing, so with that said, "Women must take charge!"

Once Upon a Time . . . in the Beginning

I know you remember the day you met your man. You told all your friends, "He's the one!" He gave you goose bumps and butterflies in your belly. There was a bliss of romance, and you looked forward to every date. You probably spent the entire week trying on clothes or shopping for new ones just to impress him. You smiled at everything he said. You put on a show for him at all times. Even if you had worked all day and just wanted to go home, take off your shoes, and plop down, if your man called to take you out, you put on those dancing shoes and twirled 'til the wee early hours of the morning. You always found time to take long weekends together somewhere romantic. You made sure you surprised him with some sexy lingerie. You probably stayed up late talking and laughing about everything and anything.

Now you have been married for quite a few years, you probably have children, and some of the romance has fizzled. You have ridden the elevator of life's ups and downs, which has steered you and your relationship into mediocrity. What a pity! The fireworks that used to light up your life when he entered your space have now lost their magic. Unfortunately, by now, some of you are on a roller-coaster

1

ride, going up and down and all around, barely hanging on. What was once fun, exciting, and exhilarating has now become more than scary or, even worse, dull. Now you just want to jump off the ride. The more the years go by, the more we sit and wonder what happened to our fairy tale romance.

Relationships sculpt us in so many ways that none of us can ever imagine or predict the outcome as we enter our lives together. Life is hard, busy, and time consuming. There is work, kids, and bills to pay. To have a successful relationship, you have to find the time every day to connect with each other, and I don't mean arguing either!

If you do have a problem, you need to ask him when there would be a good time to discuss it. Most men work all day, and the last thing they need is for you to jump right in with problems the second they walk through the door. If you let him relax first, you will find that you are much more likely to have his undivided attention. Just like you did when you were dating, you must also remember to first ask him how his day was. Make sure you listen to him as well. If he had a bad day, squeeze his hand. Give him a genuine empathetic response and understanding. Smile! Provide him the response you would appreciate in the same situation. Let him know that you care. Never take him or his work for granted, even if you feel that you are being treated that way . . . we will get to that later.

A big part of a successful relationship is in knowing when to talk about what. If your man had a horrific day, now is not a good time to pester him about the family getaway you want to plan or the garage door that needs to be repaired. When the time is more appropriate, then try to work together to find a solution that both of you can deal with. It seems obvious, but helping each other through all problems and sharing responsibilities is what makes marriages work.

Get back on to that roller coaster together, and make it fun again. Sometimes, just the little things will make our man smile. For that matter, the same is true for us. We need to be nice to each other and teach each other to always be kind. We need to remember to thank each other for things we sometimes take for granted from our partner. Of course, we never forget to say "Thank you" to strangers when they open doors for us, so why should we not say the same to the one we love? In fact, my husband still opens my car door for me. I believe he still does this because I always thank him and give him a big smile and sometimes a passionate kiss with a little show of leg. Men love to be appreciated, even for small things.

Showing appreciation is also a very easy way to train your man to do nice things for you, like getting doors or letting you go ahead of him. I often see couples together with children. A lot of times, I see the woman getting the doors or letting their kids do it. It would be a good lesson to teach your sons as well as your daughters to take with them into their adult lives. It shows a loving respect for each other and demonstrates to your children that mutual respect is desirable behavior. This is especially important for your sons. Chivalry should never die!

If you don't show appreciation, you will soon find yourself a character in one of those country "you done me wrong" songs. You will be either lost in your marriage or sadly find yourself in a divorce. Once a relationship or a marriage loses steam and boredom sets in, you must become diligent and find ways to relight the fire of romance. Divorce is just a quick call away these days, and a lot of money is lost on greedy lawyers. It is easy to walk away and blame the other, but who really gets hurt in the end? Please don't use the excuse of the kids, the bills, and how work uses up all your energy. If you do, I promise you that your marriage will suffer and your mate will, too.

Always remember that men also need to be adored just as much as we women do. But if your marriage or relationship is showing signs of flickering out, you can do things to ignite the intimacy and put the romance back into your relationship.

We are going to examine techniques and tips that the other women have successfully used to reestablish the love connection you shared with your partner when you first started dating. Maybe a weekend beach trip would spice up things. You could take a moonlit walk on the beach, stop to draw a heart in the sand, and write "I love you" inside the heart. I'm sure you can remember back when you were dating. You probably did this for at least one boy or two. And didn't you jump for joy when the boy did it for you? Wasn't it a wonderful feeling?

My husband's parents were married for sixty-seven years before my father-in-law passed away at the ripe old age of eighty-seven. I always saw them showing mutual respect for each other. In the twenty years I saw them together, I never heard one unkind word directed at the other. He still opened her car door and always let her go before him. Such chivalry! I believe that, because they found time to spend together as a couple, it made their relationship stronger, even through their life's journey of obstacles.

I used to wait for flowers to be brought to me or to be taken out for a romantic evening, but when the down economy hit, our many date nights turned into just once a week or none at all. So now I practice the "appreciating home" date night routine at least once a week, and it really does make a difference. I feel just as important as my husband does, and he has noticed how these special touches mean so much to us as a couple. I haven't yet had to pick flowers from my next-door neighbor's yard, but I would if I needed to. I have no shame, especially when it comes to romance.

2

Thou Shall Flirt

Harken back to when you first met him . . . to the moment your eyes met. Remember the way your heart jumped. Your head tilted. You gave him a smile, the come-hither look.

In case you've forgotten, it's called flirting. And you both still need it desperately. Remember the day you walked down the aisle to marry your Prince Charming? Remember the love you felt? Remember the excitement? Why then would anyone want to lose that feeling you shared on that special day? As the years go by, you may need to flirt even more. Think of it as the super glue of romance. Flirting makes the relationship stay solid so that, when life happens, the super glue can make that little crack mend and your connection become whole again.

No matter how hard you think flirting is, I promise you that it is not. You don't have to be stunningly beautiful. I'm not! In fact, I believe that flirting comes naturally to me because I love people. I love to make them smile. I love to talk, laugh, and touch, especially to the one I love. So, ladies, remember it's less painless to flirt than to get a flu shot, and it wards off much more, if you know what I mean. So don't believe the old saying, "You either have it or you don't." Trust me. You do!

First, take what I like to call "the look." Nothing makes a man feel more alive or more like a stud than that certain suggestive look he catches a woman giving him. You used to give it to him all the time when you were dating. The look first let him know you were interested in him and physically drawn to him. What a thrill it gave him then!

Well, the look will still thrill him, doubly so if he hasn't enjoyed one in years. He still craves being looked upon with desire. And you should make damn sure he's getting it from you. It will serve to remind him how sexy and virile you once found him, while reassuring him that you still do. Remember back in time when your eyes met. Think of the head tilt you most likely gave him but didn't even realize you did. Remember the sexy, sweet smile that came so innocently after? That same look is what all men want and desire because it makes them feel wanted.

Try the easiest flirtation method I use. Catch his eye, linger, and then turn away. Wait a minute, and then catch his eye again. Only this time, give him the "I want to do naughty things to you" look. Take your eyes with an "up and down the body" look, lingering at his most prized body part. Make him feel you want to eat him alive. I promise you that your man will think you are the most devastatingly beautiful woman he has ever known.

I often flirt with my husband on the phone. If you are too afraid to muster up the courage to do the face-to-face flirt, listen carefully. When my phone rings, I always check the caller ID. When I see that it is my husband, I never answer with a "hello." Instead, I say things like, "How's my handsome man?" or "It's my sexy husband!" And of course, I use my signature "sexy Marilyn Monroe voice." I sometimes say other more suggestive things, but I will leave that up to your imagination. Just flirt, flirt, and then flirt some more. Your man will love it!

Laughter Makes the Heart Grow Fonder

How often do you and your man laugh? I don't mean to imply you don't laugh, but do you still laugh together? Do you even remember the last time you both enjoyed a hearty guffaw over something funny? If not, it's time to get serious about getting humorous. It may sound strange, but a healthy stream of shared mirth and frequent laughter can reinforce the bond between lovers. It certainly helped forge that bond at the beginning. Remember when you were first dating. You laughed so much together. How you tittered and grinned at his jokes, even the stupid ones. How you listened in rapt attention to his stories, even the boring ones. Before you know it, he will push out his chest like a proud peacock, you will have just scored one thousand points with your man, and it was easy.

I once heard that laughter is the best way to keep you young. A good hearty laugh several times a day will release endorphins to the brain, which will keep you looking much younger. That, my dear friend, is a very good reason to laugh, and it is much cheaper than a face lift.

A man at any stage of his life loves to feel that he is interesting, entertaining, and funny. This is doubly true for shy or reserved men who don't have a big personality naturally. He wants and needs affirmation that he is all of these things. He wants to be the life of the proverbial party. It makes him recall the carefree attitudes and pursuits of his youth.

Is his inflated male ego at the root of this appetite? Naturally! No denials here! Unfortunately, let's be real. That fact isn't likely to change anytime soon. Thus, the wise girl makes this inherent longing in him work for her, and the canny lass turns it into a relationship plus instead of letting it become a weakness for the other woman to take advantage of when "you know who" isn't paying attention to her man. I assure you that she'll find your man uproariously funny. And that is no laughing matter! So, head off disaster by once again taking the initiative. While you may not want to create a proverbial monster by convincing him that he deserves his own sitcom, making him feel funny can be a valuable thing to your relationship, sexual or otherwise.

Men aren't as dumb as we think they are. Well, okay, some are, but they still have pretty decent powers of observation in the arena of romance. If they learned anything back in their dating days, they figured out that women love a funny guy and humor is an irresistible quality that draws women.

"What the hell do you girls see in that guy?" he and his friends would always ask in bewilderment. "He's not even good looking."

"But he's so funny!"

Men know humor is sexy to women, so it must be sexy to you. Thus, when he gets your laughter and smiles (your general interest) in response to his conversation (the way he used to), it boosts his self-confidence. It also reassures him that you're still into him after all this time. And he instinctively believes that, if he can keep you laughing and entertained, you'll stay into him.

So Much for Psychology, Now for Some Field Work

Here's one way to go about it. One evening, pour him his favorite drink to loosen him up. Pour yourself one while you're at it. Relax together in a room you don't normally share. Once you're settled and comfy, ask him to tell you a funny story or anecdote he remembers from his younger days, even before he met you. Perhaps a funny episode he had recently at work or with his cornball, accident-prone friend. Maybe you can simply ask him to tell you a joke or two.

"It's been so long since I heard a good joke!" you moan.

Some of you may feel the need to break the ice and get things going by first telling him something funny, especially if he's the shy or reserved type. No problem. You can be funny as well. Maybe now would be the time to tell him a little girl gossip about something amusing that happened to one of your girlfriends or co-workers. Men love a little gossip, too.

However you get started, once he starts to speak, lean into him, maintain eye contact, smile, and even ask for details at appropriate moments. Make him feel that you would rather listen to what he's telling you more than anything else. Even if you don't find his material particularly interesting or his jokes all that funny, humor the man. Just keep smiling and give him your full attention. Remember that the other woman would always listen to him and laugh at all his stupid, silly jokes. Now congratulate yourself. You just scored another thousand relationship points with him.

All that said, you may find yourself pleasantly surprised at the outcome of this little exercise. You may find him funnier than you expected. You may be reintroduced to that witty guy who always cracked you up during your courtship days. More importantly, you may renew all that shared laughter you enjoyed back then. Nowadays, it takes a little more encouragement to get his joke-cracker and yours cranked. Don't forget the old adage, "Laughter can keep you looking young!" Now I don't know about you, but that by itself is worth the effort!

Of course, this is a deliberate and planned opportunity for arousing his funny factor. It goes without saying (but I'll say it anyway because it's important) that you should also take advantage of the opportunities that spring up spontaneously in everyday life. A perpetually serious or stern face rarely sirs desire, his or yours. Always be quick to appreciate your man's humor with a chuckle, grin, or even well-timed "You crack me up" even when he's not consciously trying to amuse you. Trust me. He'll notice. Just keep it natural.

Your reactions, whether subtle or overt, will remind him regularly that he's clever and interesting and possesses a vibrant (and, thus, sexy) sense of humor. If you don't remind him, she's more than willing to do so. If she does, you just might find yourself alone one day. And you won't be laughing. Maybe when you get special time to dine out alone together, don't be that couple you see across the room eating and not saying a word to each other. You know what I'm talking about . . . one is reading the paper and the other is staring off into space. Be interesting. Remember some gossip to share, or make up something. Smile at him, share a bite of your food, hold his hand across the table, or sit beside him in a booth. Don't be the woman sitting there looking out into space. Just pay attention to him. Laugh!

On one of our Friday night date nights, I once asked my husband to tell me a story from his past. I admit I was a little scared of hearing a story that might involve a past girlfriend or two. The story however, was one I found very intriguing, and we ended up laughing for the entire evening as that story led to another. I could not help but notice how my husband set up and gave me the suave, debonair look, with his one arm leaning on the bar and that sexy smile that caught my eye when we first met. I found myself getting turned on, and before I knew it, I could not wait to get him home. This is one of the reasons why I married him. He always had such intriguing stories. I bet your man also has a funny story or two.

Not only is flirting fun, it can keep your self-esteem soaring off the charts. Treat flirting like your favorite game you used to enjoy when you were a little girl. If you still just can't get the picture, then try this. If you have a creative homosexual male friend, just ask him. If you don't, then borrow one! Ask him to show you his favorite flirting technique. I have a gay friend, Joey, who is a Professional ballroom dancer and hairdresser who can "flirt" me right off the planet or catwalk stage!

After all, a gay man is one of the best accessories any woman can have . . . better than any "Prada" designer bag you can purchase. Trust me on this one! An artistic gay can also give you tips on what to wear while flirting, most often, shorter skirts, tight pants, a little extra makeup, sexy high heels, and lots of "bling" (jewelry).

Flirting will keep your long-established relationship alive. I like to flirt sometimes just to make my husband laugh. Just recently, we were out shopping, and I caught him checking out this very pretty woman. Hell, she was so pretty that I was even checking her out! I smiled at him and tossed my hair, the move you sometimes see in the movies. Tilt your head to the right like you are going to touch your shoulder, but instead, take your right hand and toss your hair back. Then turn your head to the left and do the same. Then very quickly, turn your head back to the right. Pull your shoulder up with your head tilted, like you are going to kiss your shoulder, but instead, give him a pouty smile. My husband always laughs when I do this, and this lets him know I caught him, but I made a joke out of it instead of being mad.

Once when my husband and I were on a date night, we secured a secluded booth in a quaint, little Italian restaurant. We were having our wine and salad when I suddenly had to go to the ladies' room. My husband stood up to let me out of the booth because we always sit together on one side, and I was on my way. I started my little sway that I like to do to entertain my man as I walk away from him. The wine had made me lose my inhibitions.

I passed a table full of men talking like they were in a very intense meeting. As I walked by, one of the men commented on how pretty the dress I was wearing was. Another man followed suit, and they tried to strike up a conversation with me. Of course, all I had on my mind was going to tinkle, so I hurried along, just giving them a smile.

On my way back, I, of course, had to pass their table again, and not to my surprise, as you know how I feel about men and certainly the neglected ones, they again tried to engage in conversation. I just keep my eyes on my man, waiting patiently while standing by the table. I could see the smile on his face as I reached his side.

As I came close to my husband standing by the booth waiting for me, I realized how lucky I was to have a man who still had chivalry after twenty years of marriage. I stopped to give him a big, long kiss before I scooted back into the booth. That way, the men could see I was a very happy woman and my husband would be one up on the men who had just flirted with me.

My husband looked at me and said "What did those men say to you? Do I need to put them in their place?"

I just smiled and said, "No, I pretty much put them in their place already, but thanks for watching out for me!"

He replied, "Well, in that case, I have to admit that I really did enjoy your little catwalk, and I can see why you caught their attention, although it did make me a little jealous watching other men enjoying it too!"

And I have to admit, I wasn't upset at all that it made my husband jealous. It's good for him and makes me feel appreciated to know that he cares.

When I got comfortable again in the booth beside him, I reached over, grabbed his hand, and shoved it between my legs. Giving him a big smile, I whispered in his ear, "Oh Honey, you don't have anything to worry about, you're the only man I want flirting with me." I then pressed my hand in between his thighs and gently rubbed up and down on his manhood until I could feel the stiffness there. Needless to say, that little flirtation I showed to him was the start of a great evening!

The next time you have a situation where you are walking in front of your man, give him a little flirting tease walk. Get in front of him in a public place, and swing your booty to remind him of what he found sexy about you when you were first dating. And don't tell me, ladies, that you did not do that little wiggle walk for your man to tease him while you were dating. Men love to be flirted with, especially with your body language.

I once got out of the car and walked hurriedly in front of my husband because it was a very cold day and I wanted to get in where it was warm. I was wearing a very tight pair of jeans that he had earlier commented on when we were leaving the house. As I hurried along, I remembered the compliment he made when he saw me walking to the car, so I decided to flirt with him by sashaying my behind as I walked a little faster. Just when I reached the door to go inside, I turned, and looking over my shoulder, I gave him a sexy wink, stuck out my tongue, and licked my lips.

When we got inside, he grabbed my hand. "I saw your sweet, round ass moving around in those tight jeans."

"That was all you have to say," I said back to him. "Well since you were lollygagging around, I thought I would give you a little show."

I then knew I made him feel like a sexy creature with only a little flirting gesture. I then touched his manhood and rubbed it until he started to become aroused. I slowly slid my tongue into his mouth and teased the entire inside. I don't have to tell you how that little bit of flirtation ended.

I have one more word on flirting. Once when my husband was mowing our back lawn, I was inside in the cool air-conditioning, doing a little light house cleaning. I was still in my nightie. I was getting ready to spray the glass on our back door when I caught a glimpse of my husband. Not only was the poor thing sweating like someone hiking in the desert, he also looked like he was about to die of thirst. I quickly grabbed a hand towel off the kitchen sink and poured a tall glass of lemonade. As I was about to head out the door, I decided to add to this little gesture by running upstairs and putting on a sexy summer dress that I only wear around the house when I want to tease him. When I opened the door with my dress on, holding the glass of lemonade, you would not believe the smile on his face. He stopped the mower, and as I dried the sweat off his face, I gave him the lemonade. He was very appreciative as he thanked me and told me what a nice surprise this was.

Ladies, it was just a little, simple gesture that hit big with my man. I then gave him a little kiss as I thanked him for mowing the lawn.

I really do appreciate it because no way would I like that disgusting job.

You're His Other, Not His Mother

"Pick up your clothes! Put your shoes away! Take out the trash!" Now be honest. Is your man hearing the voice of your mother (or, heaven forbid, his mother) coming out of your lipstick-tinted mouth? Now be even more honest with yourself.

Do you hear it? I've heard my own mother's voice come out of my mouth plenty of times. You would think I would have learned by now. On one of my bickering sessions with my husband, I said something my mother always said in her own heated moments, and I almost stopped breathing. I really did hear my mother's voice. I was right, of course, as far as the argument went, but did he hear even one word of what I had just said?

No. I don't believe my dad ever heard a word from my mother's mouth when they would have an argument either. Why? She always used that high-pitched voice, and her words would come tumbling out of her mouth so fast that my father never really got a chance to hear what she was saying. If on a rare occasion he did hear her, he certainly never got a chance to get a word in edgewise. My mother was right most of the time, but unfortunately, she did not know how to win the fight.

This bad habit was something I had obviously brought into my own marriage(s). My mother, to her defense, learned it from her mother. We all grow up mimicking our parents to some degree, and we unknowingly bring good and bad habits into our marriages. I have worked hard in my present marriage to try not to repeat the same nagging mistakes I made in my first marriages. I only suggest you try to do the same. Also, we sometimes don't think our children are watching or listening to us. Let me make it very clear. Their little ears hear and repeat.

One of my children told me that, when he was a young boy, he would often pretend he was asleep and listen to his father and me talk or argue. You might think your little ones are asleep or occupied, playing with their toys, but they might not always be. So be careful what their little ears might be hearing. We need to be a role model for our children and model the behavior we want them to use, now and as adults. If we speak down to our husbands in a way that is demeaning or undermining their position in the household, it will be repeated in the next generation.

A man grows up consistently blocking out the nagging voice of his mother. Trust me. If he now finds himself hearing those same high-pitched irritating tones coming from you, he's now tuning you out as well. It's time to learn an important lesson. There are more subtle and infinitely more effective ways to train your loved ones to meet the reasonable expectations of daily existence around the house, for instance, a task like taking out the trash. Unless you just want to clean up after him, your aim is to get him to clean up after himself.

It's all about communication. I believe one thing we should train our husbands to do, if they don't already, is to take out the trash and pump the gas. My husband always does both. It is just not girly, and it's one thing I just will not compromise on. I, of course, clean his bathroom. I don't mind doing it, and frankly, I do a better job than my husband does. So you just have to train your man to do what is most important for you and trade off doing something he may not find fun to do. We women should never be the maid, whether we work outside the home or not. My hope for you is that, after reading this book, you will have learned to communicate more effectively with your man so you are never thought of as a nag. Instead, you're the sweet, wonderful woman he married and wanted to spend the rest of his life with until the day he dies.

Remember the goal of this book, and consider it now. Nothing is more of a turnoff to a man than a mother's nagging or critical harsh words. This means his mother, your mother, or your children's mother (you).

"But I thought men wanted to marry their mothers?" you say.

Who the heck told you that? Your mother? I thought so. Well, to be fair, Mom was both right and wrong. To clarify, a man seeks the positive attributes of his mother, not the negative. It's common sense, right? He fondly remembers her nurturing, not her nagging. He cherishes her feminine tenderness, not her testiness. He thinks of her softness, not her harshness.

"But, Karen," you respond, "it's not unreasonable to expect my husband to act like a grown-up and pick up after himself or finish his household tasks and domestic duties."

It's certainly not! It's perfectly reasonable. Nor is it wrong to verbally communicate to him that he needs to do all these simple things. You're not his mother after all, just in case you've forgotten that over the years. But (and here's the critical part) how you do this communicating can mean the difference between bitter conflict and sweet harmony.

The following few guidelines will keep you from being "the old ball and chain." He should be able to say something to you without fearing you will ridicule or reject him. Remember the golden rule, "Do unto others as you would have them do unto you." My great-grandmother (Mama Alice), a nurse and Sunday school teacher, used to tell me this all the time, and she lived to be ninety-eight years old. She was always very attentive to my grandfather, and she never raised her voice. And I mean never!

When it becomes necessary to remind your man of some task, big or small, do this:

- Take a moment to ponder how you would want to be spoken to if you were on the receiving end. In other words, choose your words and tone carefully. Nothing can whip a man into shape faster than a few wisely selected words in a sweet, soft, sexy voice.

- Strive to be informative, not accusatory. Be gentle, not confrontational. Instead of "You didn't pick up your shoes," try a calmer, less combative approach. "Honey, you forgot to pick up your shoes. Can you please put them away for me?" Even when you just want to pick them up and hurl them at his head, just take a deep breath and smile.

- Add an encouraging kiss to sweeten the deal, and promise a reward for later, like "I promise to give you a back rub later." Or promise him something you know he enjoys. Wouldn't that be a nice trade-off and a faster way to get things done? It's all about communication. How you communicate makes all the difference in getting tasks done. Think about when you ask your children to pick up things or clean their rooms. You sometimes use a little encouragement and offer a reward, so why can't you do the same for your husband?

To try another tack, pick up the shoes yourself on occasion and later say, "Sweetie, I saw you forgot to put away your shoes, so I did it for you." This subtle notification of what you've done for him can shame him into better behavior next time. At this point, you've accomplished a couple things. You've gently reminded him that he's been slack in something he already knows he's supposed to do, and you've let him know that there's been a consequence that has, unfortunately, fallen on you. If nothing else, you've shown your love for him with a simple gesture. Remember, the little things mean a lot.

Of course, you can also try a little reverse psychology. Thank him before he does something he's supposed to. "Thanks for putting away your shoes, sweetie pie. I really do appreciate your help. It sure makes cleaning the house a lot faster." This also applies to his shirt, the wet towel, and his underwear he has left on the floor that he thinks will magically be put away. Whichever strategy you adopt, gentle admonishment or subtle shame, you've successfully avoided the overt motherly nagging that makes him cringe in repulsion. It's a true attraction killer for any man.

Now, what if he, lo and behold, starts getting it right? And gets it right consistently? It's not rocket science, girlie. You reward him often and well. His reward can take many forms: a kiss, a compliment, his favorite dish, or a kind word that lets him know that you notice and are pleased when he fulfills his obligations and takes his responsibilities seriously. It can even prove effective to appeal to his natural male competitiveness. Say things like, "It's so nice to have a sweet husband who picks up after himself. Jennifer's husband expects her to mother him. He's like a helpless little boy and so inconsiderate of her." Or maybe, "Thank heaven I've got a man who's capable of looking after his own needs. That's so rare these days." Or even a simple, "Thanks for being a sweetheart and picking up after yourself."

Even a simple statement made in front of friends when the occasion presents itself ("I am such a lucky lady that my husband always picks up after himself, and it sure makes my life around the house easier") is a great example of a small compliment that can pay off later in a big way.

Don't you love it when your man compliments you in front of friends? Whatever words you choose, lead him to the understanding that you view his self-reliance and individual initiative around the house as inextricably linked to his masculinity and strength of character, not to mention to his sexiness. Real men can and do see to their own simple domestic needs. And men who do this, he must learn, make you hot. Personally, I see nothing wrong with using his male ego, including his innate desire to outperform other men, against him. In the sweetest way possible, of course!

My husband and I were once at a party, and the conversation led to housework, among other things. I declared how lucky I was to have a husband who always picks up after himself. You would have thought I had bragged about how good he is in bed. Not only did he give me the sweetest smile, he was extra attentive to me for the rest of the day. The other women began complimenting him and even started telling him how much they wished their husbands would do the same. Men love when other women take notice. This is one time I did not mind.

Of course, one reward highly likely to make an impression on your burgeoning domestic Hercules is you. To be specific, you in the bedroom. To be even more specific, you in the bed in the bedroom, that is, you naked in the bed in the bedroom. This is certainly one reward that will teach him to help out around the house.

In anticipation of all these pleasant rewards, verbal or physical, that man of yours just might begin looking forward to pleasing you. Maybe you can say something like, "Now that the housework is done and I have some "us" time, let's go unmake the bed!" Men, you see, are much like Pavlov's dogs. Positive reinforcement is the key to forming positive habits and facilitating good behavior. Of course, there are manifold other ways we can compare men to dogs (the drooling, the periodically eating something off the floor, their preclusion to shamelessly beg while giving us that pathetic "puppy dog in the pet shop window look" and by the way of a sad apology for all they have done wrong in the past and all the transgressions we know they will commit in the future) but we'll defer those for now.

To conclude, the above anti-nagging principles apply to much more significant things than putting away of shoes. They can be applied with great success to all the commitments and responsibilities of your shared life and relationship. After all, you are not his mother. You're the sweet bride he married. You are supposed to be his partner, his best friend. Don't let counterproductive nagging douse his passion for you. It just might drive him to the arms of the other woman.

Of course, all couples fight, and no matter how hard you try, it is inevitable that conflict will arise. When these occasions occur, think before you speak. Count to five, and ask yourself if what has happened is really worth the time and emotional turmoil an argument will cost. Are you dealing with a habit he refuses or is unable to break, or was what happened just a fluke? Remember to choose your battles, another lesson my great-grandmother taught me.

While we're on the subject of choosing, you will also want to choose how you approach your man when attempting to communicate with him about an argument or issue. A psychologist once advised me against ever starting a sentence with the word "you" when arguing with a man. Men will automatically shut down and not even hear anything else you have to say, focusing their minds instead on building their defenses to win the dispute. She told me to begin your sentences with "I." For example, instead of starting with saying, "You really made me mad," try the less aggressive statement, "I really feel bad because I wanted . . ." You will be pleasantly surprised to see what a difference a little rewording can make. From that day forward, I have always started my sentences with "I," "me," or anything but "you." Believe me. It really has worked. I don't have to follow him up the stairs anymore trying to get my point across. I also, as she told me, ask first if this is a good time to talk.

Men seem to keep a lot of things to themselves. They don't open up and tell all like we women do. So we need to train our man to open up. We need to be able to talk about what is on our minds and not be afraid that the other will reject us. If you keep your thoughts to yourself, especially the negative ones, it puts a barrier between you and your happiness in your relationship. Negativity breeds negativity. The lack of communication leads to a breakdown of a good marriage, especially if your thoughts like being jealous after seeing him talk to another woman at a party or if he gets really angry at you for spending too much money on that dress you purchased. It can sometimes be a trivial thought that, left not discussed together, can often later be blown out of proportion.

It takes a lot of practice to learn that your differences first brought you both together. Not only do I believe that communication is vital, it helps us maintain our separate individuality. In my second marriage, I could not understand this so it eventually led to me needing more than he could give without losing his own individuality, thus adding to the breakdown of our marriage. When we marry, sometimes we believe we actually have to become one. We must remain somewhat separate so we can maintain our own personality. Remember, that is what first attracted us to each other. These differences will give your marriage the vitality and delights that will undoubtedly make your relationship an opportunity to grow and allow each of you to enjoy your individual experiences together.

Remember the Cleavers

Remember the Cleavers? Wouldn't it be nice if we could all greet our husband at the door when he comes home from work? Wouldn't it be great if we had the time to cook dinner from scratch every night? Well, we can do things for our husbands when he gets home.

This might not be the way June Cleaver did it, but try some little things and see what a difference it will make to spice things up. Women with children can do these things when they can't really find the time to do other more time-consuming things they might like to do.

Appreciating Home

1. **Vent someplace else (or to someone else).** When we have a bad day, most of us go home and vent to our husbands. Before we know it, we have gone on and on about something that our man could really care less about. Chances are, he might have also had a bad day. Even though this is the hardest thing not to do, we seem to tell our husbands way too much. So next time, ladies, call your girlfriend, and vent

to her. Or call your mom or sister. Call anybody. Just let it all out. Not only will you feel better getting all that negative stuff off your chest and venting your frustrations, it will not be at the expense of your man.

2. **Put on something pretty and comfortable.** When you get home and want to get into something comfortable, please, ladies, put on something pretty and comfortable. Even if you have children, there is nothing wrong with putting on a pretty, long gown and matching robe. Yes, jogging clothes are more comfortable, so you say, but not so pretty or feminine. Isn't that what you want your husband to see when he looks at you? Pretty. You don't have to do this every day, mind you, but at least once or twice a week would really make a difference. I can't tell you how many men feel they are taken for granted because their wives used to wear pretty things. She used to put on makeup and on and on. For thirty years, I've heard this from men while they are shopping. It also teaches your children that wearing pretty lingerie is perfectly okay and, yes, acceptable. While I'm on the subject, ladies, please color your lips for that kiss hopefully your husband will be receiving from you when he walks in the door from work. It only takes a second to apply it, and isn't your man worth that time? A little mascara can also go a long way and only takes a minute to put on. And what a difference it makes!

3. **Light a candle.** When you serve dinner, even if you have children, there is no reason you can't make it a romantic one once in a while. Light a candle, put it close to your husband, and let him know that you lit it for him. The scent will be a nice addition and sets a more relaxing mood. Go outside in your yard and pick some flowers for the table. Maybe that will remind your man to bring home flowers once in a while. You also could pick up a small bouquet at the local grocery store.

4. **Set the table.** Once in a while, use your best china and the good napkins, too. Nothing says "you're special" quite like setting a nice table for the man you love.

5. **Prepare the bed.** Before you go to bed, turn your husband's side of the bed down for him and fluff up his pillows. Try spraying just a bit of your favorite perfume on his pillow. I promise you that he will take notice and it will make him feel special. You will also enjoy all these things and put you both in the mood to appreciate each other. It really only takes a few extra minutes to show you care, and isn't your relationship worth it?

6. **Make time for a quickie.** If you and your man always seem to run out of time to have a long sexual encounter, then I strongly encourage you to make time for a quickie. They don't always have to result in an orgasm. They can just be a fun way to tease him and keep his fantasies with you in mind. To execute a good quickie, you only need just a few minutes. It's been shown that afternoon delights are just that because sex drive is at its highest. Call your man, and tell him to meet you at home for a snack. If he cannot leave work and time allows you, go pick him up, and drive him around the block. Find a parking lot, park in a secluded area, cover yourself with a blanket, and let him put his hands under it. Let him touch you for a while until he gets to breathing hard, and enjoy a few moments together. Another great spot is to find a restaurant where there is only one small single bathroom. Grab your man, and lock the door. Just the danger of getting caught in a public place releases the same adrenalin that it produces when you are having an orgasm, so it is a great tool for foreplay. Men get excited just because it is sex out of the norm, so all they need is just a little more visual, like a peek at your bra. You don't have to get all the way undressed. Just wear something you can pull or slide down a little. Then grab his hands and shove them down your top or panties. Just a little romp in the hay, as my grandpa used to say, and

it will leave a lasting impression on your man. Don't forget to talk dirty. Instead of your usual groans or request, tell him what to do in a more authoritative voice. Try a little tongue instead of a kiss, and remember, if you can't get off on a quickie, then do it for him. This is an incredible experience for you to give to your man and something you can take to the bedroom for some sexy conversation later. Quickies will let your man know that you can be in charge of a good time. Also, it can be a fun game to play of just finding unusual places to have one. So the next time you're not in the mood and he is, try a quickie, and experience the delight of having a brief, spontaneous episode of sexual activity. You might just have him eating out of your hands, and won't that be fun? Here are some examples of places to have quickies, just in case you need a little encouragement:

- In a closet in his office
- On the backseat of a public bus (making sure you are wearing a full skirt)
- In the ocean with people just a few feet away (hanging on to a raft together and letting the tide disguise what you are really doing)
- In the parking lot of a grocery store (making sure you are parked far enough away)
- Under a blanket behind a tree in the park
- In a stall in a (clean) public restroom
- The next time you are stuck in traffic in rush hour (a great time for a blow job)
- After hours on a golf course or cemetery (if you are not afraid of ghosts)

Use your best judgment here, and try not to get arrested for indecent exposure.

5

Is Your Relationship Out of Sync?

Has your relationship seemed out of sync lately? To be specific, does your man seem out of sync sexually lately? Does his sex drive seem a bit stalled? Does he seem a little uninterested in the bedroom, not performing things you usually enjoy?

If so, no doubt you're riddled with self-doubts, endless self-analysis, and tortuous self-questioning. We women are masters of that. Why is his desire so dull? Is it me? Is he no longer attracted to me? Does he no longer find my body physically appealing? Is he angry at me? Is he sleeping with someone else? Before you reach any of these conclusions and join a sex anonymous group, set up weekly appointments with a shrink, or decide just to hire a private detective, stop and consider a few things first.

Men have a lot on their minds these days, just like you and every other woman. They feel life's pressures and its manifold responsibilities, as fully as we do. To complicate matters for them, however, they also feel constrained to be the strong one in the relationship, family, and household. They're taught at a young age that "big boys don't cry." As a result, they often keep their emotions and uncertainties bottled up and don't feel at liberty to open up and confide in their partners like women do. Often, their reluctance to communicate and share their feelings stems from a genuine fear of upsetting you.

Sometimes, they wish to avoid appearing weak or inadequate. Being needy isn't manly after all, and they don't want to appear so. This problem is why a lot of men keep things to themselves. It also often fosters or coincides with a lack of enthusiasm in the bedroom. When life is sometimes stressing them out, they're just not in the mood. Yes, even men sometimes aren't in the mood. Not only does this manifest itself in his general lack of interest in sex, it also appears in his ability to perform as well. And for God's sake, don't ever point out that his pride and joy looks like a limp dishrag.

So how do you coax him out of this staleness and lack of sexual interest? Don't ask your man "What's wrong?" while you're in bed and he either seems uninterested or unable. Instead of assuming that it must be something wrong with you, try to determine, with kind inquiries and understanding, what is at the root of his worries or disinterest. If he's not in the mood for love, don't pressure him. He's just out of sync. And don't take it personally. He may, at that moment, need something other than sex. To be specific, he might need your undivided attention, empathy, and willingness to listen if he wants to talk about himself. We women can be attention hogs. Let him talk. As he does, be a good listener. He may just need a sympathetic ear. Or he may not want or need to talk at all. He may just need a hug or cuddle and the reassuring presence of his most beloved friend. Remember, men want and need the same attention we do.

If he does seem open to discussing what's bothering him, let him share at his own pace and in his own way. You don't have to talk or give an immediate opinion on everything he says. He may just need to get things off his chest. (And sometimes that may include you.)

Also, let him know frequently that you appreciate and respect him for everything he does, like going to work even when he's sick. He is being a good provider, a good husband and father, and a good lover. He remembers your birthday and anniversary (well, he'd better!). Praise him for both the big and little things, like taking out the trash, filling up your car with gas, and washing the dishes. I'm sure you thank your girlfriends when they do things for you so why not thank the man you married.

So don't think it has something to do with you because he's out of sync. It could just mean that life has him down, not up, right now.

Things They All Do (Men)

Does your man or husband surf the tube but automatically stop when young, sexy girls are romping around in the sand in string bikinis? Do you go to bed before him and wake up an hour later to find him still watching adult TV? Have you ever been out in public and saw his head turn when another sexy woman walks by? If you answered yes to any or all of these questions, then you need to ask yourself what he's getting from them that he's not getting from you. Chances are, you have neglected the little boy in him or maybe the attention that every man needs, especially as they get older. You might try the following things:

- The next time he stops on the bikini romp channel, go put on yours. Grab a blanket and some oil, and get down on the floor. Start putting the oil on the inside of your legs, and ask him if he would like to help. I'm sure he won't hesitate. That will certainly take his mind off the channel he was watching.
- The next time he's up late watching adult TV, sit beside him, and watch with him. You'll be surprised how turned on you'll get along with him. It also is a good way to learn new things. As for the head turning, you could knock his head off, or you can take a more gentle and loving approach and grab his attention by taking his hand and giving him a sexy smile. Remind him how hot he is. That will stop him dead in his tracks. Maybe even point out a few attractive women for him. Let him look a little. I bet he won't be so eager to

stare the next time. This could be a little game you both play together. It might just turn you on. It will for sure show him how confident you are in yourself. To men, this is very sexy.

How to Weather the Storm

All relationships, no matter how perfect they are, will fall into deep waters at one point. It's like being on a sailboat, basking in the beautiful sunshine together with a cocktail in your hands, and feeling like life just can't get any better when, out of nowhere, the skies turn dark and the winds start to rock your boat. The boat sways so harshly from side to side until everything gets really scary. The only way you can survive this rocky turmoil is to work together as a team. Hold tightly together on those sails so they don't get ripped off. Pretty soon, the sun will shine again, and you will be able to once again lie back together and enjoy the rest of the ride. If you don't decide to work together when the tides get rough, you may find yourself with the boat tipped over. You are both over your heads without a life jacket in very deep, dark, scary waters with lots of man-eating sharks.

When you go through an unhappy period in your relationship, remember the contract you signed. In today's world, it's the one contract that is easiest to break. We get married, and we buy a house, an expensive car, and furniture. Then most of us birth our precious babies. Sometimes life takes us down a less romantic road, so I hope the suggestions in this book will help you to work harder on your marriage and not give up. Just remember that no marriage is perfect. Communication is the key.

6

Lovemaking or Sex?

S ex is important in any relationship. Yes, I know you've heard that a thousand times. TV and magazines have told you. No doubt, your husband has told you. While I certainly agree with that assertion, however frequently quoted, I must make my own little addendum. Sex is important in a relationship, but lovemaking is the very crux of romantic intimacy. It has the power to bind two people together emotionally in a way mere sex can never do.

Sex is the union of two bodies. Lovemaking is the union of two bodies, two hearts, two souls, and two beings into one person. Sex is an act. Lovemaking is an act. Lovemaking also is an occasion celebrating and magnifying your love for another person.

Sex may or may not involve planning and time. Lovemaking takes thoughtful mental and emotional preparation, the unselfish giving of your time and faculties, your best energies, to your partner and to the act itself. Sex at any time, in any form, consists of give-and-take to some degree, great or small. Lovemaking is giving all of yourself and receiving all your lover offers in return.

Sex has a tendency or risk to focus on oneself first and foremost. True lovemaking brooks no such self-centered appetites. It rather prefers to fulfill your partner's needs and desires as much or more than your own. Sex gives you pleasure. During lovemaking, you derive enjoyment and satisfaction in your lover's physical and emotional pleasure as well as your own.

It also requires time in the calendar and schedules in every sense of the word. A couple should be ashamed of going more than thirty days without a sensual night of unhurried, non-stressed sex. I believe that having a night of lovemaking should be on everyone's priority list. Make the time. Your relationship will be worth the effort.

Lovemaking is freeing your inner sexuality to the utmost. This, especially for women, is possible only where there is full commitment, security, and trust in the relationship itself. Sex can include any or all of the five senses in the experience. Good lovemaking incorporates them all: taste, smell, sight, sound, and touch, the entire body and mind. If you and your man have lost your emotional connection, you need to reawaken these five senses.

- **Taste:** Use edible lotions, give each other long massages, and lick the (edible) lotion off.
- **Smell:** Take bubble baths together. Rub edible chocolate body paint on his back, and write dirty words. If he can guess the word, you can give him the prize. After you get out and dry off, don't forget to wear his favorite perfume. I had a customer once tell me that she takes a whore's bath when she is in a hurry. While I am not quite sure what that means, she also told me another time that her husband does everything right and rocks her world but does not perform oral sex on her. I can only wonder why.
- **Sight:** Wear sexy lingerie. Need I say more?
- **Touch:** Use your imagination to play with fur, feathers, and ice cubes, I am sure you could find something exciting to do with them!
- **Sound:** Talk seductively, softly, and sexy instead of your usual everyday voice.

Remember the quote from *Forrest Gump*? "Life is like a box of chocolates. You never know what you're gonna get." Make your love a box of chocolates!

Turn Up the Heat

And I don't mean on your furnace! Working late at night or chasing after your children all day can certainly put a damper on your sex drive. There are aphrodisiacs that are natural and perfectly safe to help you get your mojo on again:

- **Anything made with peppermint.** Try soaps or shampoos with peppermint. They have a stimulating cooling effect on your clitoris. For a little kinky fun and something a little different, take a piece of peppermint candy and suck on it for a minute. Lean in like you are going to give him a big kiss, and ask him to open his mouth. Drop the piece of candy into his mouth, and then tell him to take it to and from his mouth to your clitoris. Not only will the peppermint stimulate your clitoris, it will make you taste as sweet as candy.
- **Topical gels.** Make sure you find a topical gel with menthol and arginine in the ingredients. They are warm and tingly to the clitoris and increase the blood flow to the area. I personally enjoy and recommend Liquid V.
- **Natural herbs.** Use some natural herbs to help stimulate you. You must take them on a regular basis. Ginkgo biloba is a good one, but it needs to be forty to eighty milligrams with 24 percent ginkgo heterosides in it and should be taken twice every day. Saw palmetto needs to be one hundred and sixty milligrams with at least 85 percent fatty acid, and it is also taken twice daily. Both these herbs are recommended for women as well as men.
- **Pumpkin seeds**—Now I know that most everyone has heard of letting slimy oysters slide down your throat to get you horny. But if you don't like the feel of something

slimy, (the thought of them gives me the hebie jeebies) Try eating pumpkin seeds, a great snack and not full of calories. They are proven to get your engine started or your motor running.

Romance: The Ultimate Aphrodisiac

If you like Pina Coladas,
And gettin' caught in the rain. If you like the feel of the ocean and the
Taste of champagne
Looking for romantic ideas? Take a cue from Rupert Holmes. He sang "Escape (The Piña Colada Song") *It starts out like this . . .*

I was tired of my lady, we've been together too long
Like a worn out recording of my favorite song
So, while she lay there sleeping, I read the paper in bed.
In the personal columns, there was this ad that I read . . .
There really are women who put ads in various papers, and the men who read them, married or single, rarely stop at just reading these ads. Some will eventually give in to curiosity and temptation and respond to one (or more) of them. So let's ward off women like that and put an ad in your husband's brain. A really sexy idea that he won't soon forget. Maybe he'll be reminded of it every time there is a rainy day. So here's a little adventure you can take with your man.

Next time there's a soft summer rain (not a thunderstorm . . . unless that turns you or him on), pour a glass of champagne, and tell your man you want to take a stroll. Trust me. This won't be just any stroll. First, to maximize the experience (and this is important) you'll need to dress for the occasion. Don something lightweight and feminine. You know, something that will cling, especially when it gets damp. Of course, the traditional favorite, guaranteed to drive men wild, is a white cotton dress, or just a white T-shirt with a full flouncy skirt (I'll explain later why the "flounce".) Remember the wet t-shirt contests they always have at the beach? Men LOVE them! You just can't keep them away!

Now that you're appropriately attired for your romantic outing, it's time to conveniently forget your umbrella and—drum roll, please—your underwear. For good measure, you can leave the bra at home, too. And don't go telling me you feel so naked without it. You're not naked. You're almost naked.

That's the image you want to keep burning in his head during this outdoor adventure. Why the flouncy skirt? Bring a camera along. It can be fun to stop and let your man take some sexy, provocative pictures of you. Men love sexy pictures. That's why Hugh Hefner is so filthy rich.

Now, take his hand and set out. Choose a scenic route that is as private as possible. Otherwise, be sure you're dressed modest enough for public view. Think trees, grass, and meadow. If the terrain is accommodating, shed your shoes at some point and walk barefoot. (Make sure that your toes are polished since men love pretty feet.)

Now go back to your walk. Savor the feel of the falling rain on your hair and skin. Feel it soak into your clothes and the chill bumps you are now getting as the rain drips down your breasts. Let him see your top clinging to your curves. This will entice him to the marrow. You might mention that your nipples are hard from the cool dampness. Of course, he's probably already noticed this, but you'll enhance the thrill for him by saying it aloud. (Men love dirty talk.) If you're not comfortable being so verbally blunt, use whatever words or gestures you like. The point, no pun intended, is to draw attention to them.

Try to find a place to sit or lay, maybe a grassy spot beneath some trees. Tell your man you need a little break. When he sits down beside you, take his hand and place it on one of your breasts. Then tell him to lie back and relax. Climb on and give him an even better look at what lies on top of him. This could also be the time you look up into his eyes and give him not only that sultry smile but also a long, passionate kiss. While the rain is sprinkling down, this makes your bodies wet. Get his sexual appetite wet.

After you smooch a little, lie down in his lap so he gets his eyes full and tell him how much you love him and how sexy he looks in the rain. Give him a long, sexy kiss with a little tongue this time. Make it one that he will remember for a long time, most especially the next time he has to take a trip out of town on business. Memories can last forever if they are good ones. One day, you'll be sitting on the porch in your rocking chairs and reflect back on your times together, saying, "Honey, remember the time . . ." And he'll say, "Oh, yeah . . ."

On your walk home, make sure you hold hands. Take time to give him a few smiles. If you pass a rosebush, stop and pick one and give it to him. Men love flowers, too. Or drop it down the front of your top and ask him to smell it. Maybe this would be a good time to strike a sexy pose.

When you get close to home, casually say in a sexy, sultry voice that you might need his help in pulling off your drenched clothes, one task you definitely won't have to nag him about. I think you know how to proceed from there. Wink.

Who knew getting caught in a summer rain could be so exciting? (This is why you see this little skit in so many movies) It's hot and sexy. If you're still shy about this delightful sort of excursion into the great romantic outdoors, try envisioning the other woman taking this wet stroll with your man. Does that help?

Have fun drying off, or stay wet. Either way, enjoy your playtime together!

Real-Life Story

Star, one of my most fun, carefree customers, is divorced with two boys. She has decided to not let the rest of her life be as boring as her marriage was. She told me she takes half the blame for their breakup because they used to do so many fun things when they first dated, but as they had children, she focused more on them, and the fun soon became a part of the past. This is another example of things we do when we first marry. We choose each other because of all the fun things we did together, like the vacations and games we played, but then life comes along, and we just don't focus on what really is the most important priority.

Star loves to take her boyfriend out in the wild and dance naked under the moonlight. They take vacations together in nudist camps or topless beaches. Even though she has two young boys who used to keep her tired and bogged down with homework and life, she has decided to sign them up for camp, music lessons, and sports so she can enjoy some of her life as well. She reminds me of a flower child. She dresses in long Bohemian skirts and never wears panties, and she lives her life in a carefree way. Star lives life to its fullest, and you can, too.

So ladies, don't let your children keep you from a sexy stroll in the rain with the man you love!

7

Hey, Cinderella! Sex Is Not a Chore (If It Is, You're Doing Something Wrong)

In storybooks, one gets the impression that the post-wedding sex will be fresh every morning and every night. Those of us who inhabit the real world know better. Of course, the prince is never overworked, and Cinderella is never inundated with the royal laundry. Having an army of servants and assorted underlings certainly helps the royal "biatch" hold on to the passion.

After years of dating or marriage, sex can become the same-ol'-same-ol'. It can be difficult to break free of our routines and ruts, however pleasurable, intimate, and necessary they may remain in and of themselves. But it's important and rewarding to make occasional changes and additions to mix it up a little.

Think of your favorite song. Now think of it playing every time you turn on the radio. You'd soon be heartily bored of that song. It's the same with sex. It shouldn't always be the same. It should expand, grow, and explore, and in the process, it will deepen the feeling of intimacy between the two of you.

So how do you add some new tunes to your sexual repertoire? Become a duet making sweet music together:

- **Add a little spice now and again.** Get yourself in a kinky mood by finding the nearest adult bookstore, and go directly to the erotica section. Select a book together, and take it home (in your excitement, don't forget to pay for it!). Sit together, and take turns reading aloud from it. The "voice" is perfect for this sort of auditory titillation. A little lingerie and candlelight can definitely enhance the mood. Who knew literature could hold such exciting rewards? If you are afraid to visit the local bookstore, make sure you check one out the next time you both go out of town. It can really make for a more exciting vacation, too.

- Banish forever the following poisonous phrases and all similar excuses from your vocabulary:

    - "I don't have the time to spice up my sex life." Find time. Chances are, the other woman has plenty of time to devote to your man's desires. Just think of all the free time you'll have on your hands should he leave you for some other woman.

    - "My job consumes all my energy. When I get home, I'm too tired to feel romantic." Get romantic. You owe it to yourself and your partner. If job-related demands and concerns are keeping you from maximizing your sexual enjoyment and intimacy with him, something's wrong. (There's also a good chance your relationship is suffering in other ways, too.) You weren't too tired for him while you were dating. I'm sure you were working a full-time job then too, right? Maybe somehow he's slipped on the priority list. If you have to, change jobs, (easier than divorce and changing husbands). Reassess your commitments. If you ever fake it, this is the time. Faking it with him might be better than not giving him any time at all. Think of it this way. Plenty of single and lonely married women are just around the corner, maybe in his office, in the grocery store, or, heaven forbid, next door, just waiting to pick up for your lack of time. Heaven forbid things escalate and you find yourself divorced. Sadly, you will then find all the time you need, the time you don't want to find.

- "My kids keep me so busy." Get them busy for a change. Don't let kid time be a constant drain/ intrusion on your spouse time, including sexual enjoyment. Make what changes you need to your schedule and theirs. Pop in movie. Buy a new game. Send them outside for two hours. Let them play with the neighbor's children. Maybe you can talk with a close friend, and the two of you can swap children for an afternoon or trade a sleepover night, giving you the whole night to spend with your man without interruption. These are just a few suggestions, but you get the idea. In other words, don't use your kids as an excuse for not maintaining a healthy, vibrant sex life. It may take a little planning and a little reorganization, but isn't it worth it? After all, it is an investment in your relationship, one you want to maintain after the kids are gone and living lives of their own. If you allow the intimacy to drain out of your marriage now, imagine what your life will be like once you and your husband become empty nesters.

Let your children revolve around you and your marriage, not the other way around. If you allow it, they can be a constant claim on your time and all your energy, which is harmful to your relationship with you and your spouse.

When I was a young girl, my mother would pop in a Disney movie and give us four children a bowl of popcorn. If we even hinted that we did not want to sit and watch the movie, she would tell us that we could go to our rooms and take a nap because that is what she and Dad were going to do. Of course, we, not wanting to take a nap, jumped at the idea of movie and popcorn. We never suspected they were doing anything else but napping, so try it. That should at least free up ninety minutes for you.

I'm not saying your children are not important, but even the Bible says to put God first and your husband second. That means children are after your husband's needs. A customer once shared with me that her husband looks at her but doesn't see her anymore. When he talks, he uses the word "me" instead of "us." She felt they had stopped being "us," and that was starting to scare her.

My belief is that you are sometimes so busy being a mother that you lose yourself and may not even realize it has happened until a slap in the face awakens you. Your children are gone, and your husband doesn't even notice you anymore.

"Why?" you ask yourself.

Real-Life Story

I will try to use my customer Miranda as an example as to why I think men do that. I believe she is a mother who has let herself get lost in motherhood, but not on purpose. She, like so many mothers, dresses like a soccer mom most of the time with hair pulled back in a ponytail and no makeup. I think that, before she realized it, she put her daughter first and her husband second.

Recently, she and her husband were invited to a function. She went into her closet to find something to wear and realized she had nothing new. But she did have a lot of shorts and jogging attire. She, like a lot of mothers, had not shopped for herself in quite some time. She freaked out for a while and then decided to come to Karen's Beautiful Things to find the perfect outfit. She heard, of course, that we could dress her in style and all in a New York minute. Her function was that night. Of course, not only did she come to the right place, we helped her play dress-up for over an hour. It was so much fun. She kept saying she was so used to wearing jogging clothing that she didn't feel like herself. We kept playing dress-up until my son Brian and I got her just the right things that complemented her body. I really believe she had as much fun as we did. She kept saying that, not only did she have fun, she felt so girly and had not experienced that in such a long time that she could not wait to see how her husband would react to seeing her in such pretty things. Miranda is such a pretty woman and just let herself get wrapped up into mommyhood that she lost track of herself. I can honestly say that she left with a fresh attitude, along with new clothes.

The next time I saw her, she told me that, when she got ready for the event, she could not believe how her husband really took notice of how different and feminine she looked. He paid extra attention to her all evening and even held her hand. Instead of the usual pair of shorts and T-shirt, she put on one of the outfits she purchased from us. Not only did she feel pretty, even her friends took notice.

This is another example of women with children who never buy themselves pretty things because they put their children first. Miranda's husband is a pilot and travels overnight, and he is with beautiful women at least four days a week. I believe that, when he returns home, she should greet him at home while wearing something feminine, not her usual attire. Remember, the other woman would never take him for granted, and that is why it is very important to keep the spark alive. I believe Miranda should wear whatever the heck she wants while her husband is on his four-day trips, but when he comes home, it is time to retire those frumpy clothes and don something feminine. Just think. He is gone too many days with too many women, and she should not take him for granted. This goes for your man, too. If you start seeing him in worn and tattered clothes, buy him something new to wear for you. Remember, most men are not shoppers. So make sure your man has some new digs, too.

Wearing pretty things and not lounging clothes all the time can really make you feel better about yourself, too. It is a win-win situation.

Real-Life Story

Roslyn, a good customer, once came in to buy some lingerie. She told me how long it had been since she even purchased anything for herself, much less lingerie. She and her husband had just divorced, and she was just starting to date again so she wanted to be prepared. She did admit how often her husband hinted for her to wear lingerie, but she was always too tired or had to take care of the boys and just neglected his needs. Now, here she was, in my shop. She apparently had found time now to buy lingerie for her new boyfriend. She admitted to me that she should have listened to her husband and "bought some damn lingerie" because now she was buying it, divorced and really past the dating age. She had been thrown into this lifestyle.

She admitted to me that she got married young and had been married for fifteen years, so she didn't even know how to date in this world we now live in. I could only feel bad for her, her ex-husband, and her boys now growing up in a divorced home. Too bad she had to lose her husband to the other woman to finally find the time to purchase lingerie.

Her husband confessed after the divorce that he was very sorry and asked her forgiveness but felt he was always being taken for granted. He told her she stopped wearing makeup unless she was going to work and mostly wore lounging clothes around the house. So he let himself stray to take care of his own fantasies and personal needs. This is such a sad story with a drastic ending when maybe it could have been different. Ladies, I have heard so many stories like this. If your husband is constantly asking you for something, it's time to take notice.

8

Pretty Woman

Remember the scene in *Pretty Woman* in which Richard Gere takes Julia Roberts on a shopping spree? Do you recall his big grin as he watches Julia try on clothes, happily anticipating seeing what she'd have on the next time she exited the dressing room?

That scene should provide some inspiration for you to inject a little high-fashion romance into your love life, without the paparazzi and anorexia. And no, your man does not have to be filthy rich. Nor do you even have to leave home. Nor do you have to look like Julia Roberts. But remember, men are visual creatures. Thus, again, we are wise to appeal to our man's optic nerve and brain.

It's simple. Just sit him down in his favorite chair with his favorite drink, and instruct him to sit back and enjoy the show. Play some good runway or high-energy dance music while you strut your stuff. Anything with a good beat will do. (Even something peppy from the movie.) Oh, here's another bit of housekeeping we need to do. Be sure your thermostat is set at a comfortable, lingerie-friendly temperature.

Now here's the catch. You won't actually be modeling clothes for him. This private fashion show will consist of you modeling lingerie. Sexy lingerie, I needn't tell you. No granny panties!

Of course, the first article of fashion you'll don is "the look." Immediately pin him down with it, and don't let him go until the show is over and/or he's swept you up in his arms and is racing to the bedroom.

Each time you exit your dressing room in a new lingerie ensemble, pretend you are a runway model. Put your shoulders back with your breasts forward. Take a few twirls around the room, and really strut your stuff. Thrust your hip out to one side and then the other, making sure you let your booty sway as you turn to walk away. Stop at some point, looking over your shoulder and pouting in a little sexy model-like fashion.

This is a good spot to suggest an idea for an intermission to the show. Maybe stop, bend over, and touch your toes. Or just bend over, showing him a little of what is to come. I'm sure you can come up with a little intermission of your own.

At some point, when he least expects it, go sit on his knee or lap (or even straddle him) and pleasure him with a long French kiss. Then kiss his neck with light feather kisses. It's sad but true. Couples who have been together for years often deny themselves this sort of long, languorous, romantic epic kiss. (A quick little peck is definitely not enough here.) Well, now is the time to renew this simple treasure.

Wait. Simple? Did I say simple? The kiss is the beginning and end of the expression of mutual desire and intimate love. There's a reason it costs more to kiss a prostitute. Further explanation would be superfluous here. All I will say is do it and watch things intensify to a whole new level of passion. Few things can out-sexy the simple kiss.

Remember, as you are giving him that hot tamale kiss, press into him with as much of your body parts you can. You know which ones I mean, the ones he loves to touch when he gets a chance.

Okay, back to the show. You have now left him wanting more. And you have more lingerie to show him. Of course, you have purchased several outfits, haven't you? Only one would be such a shame, especially now that he is waiting for a show.

Now, if you have a creative nature or, specifically, a knack for photography, place a camera (film optional) near his chair beforehand. With your eyes, indicate suggestively that he can take pictures of you in sultry poses as you sport your various outfits. Maybe he has, at one time or another, even fantasized about being the photographer at a modeling shoot. So smile for the camera. Any particularly good shot can be framed and given as a future anniversary present or as an unexpected morning surprise tucked in his workday briefcase. Think about it. He's at his office expecting nothing, and all of a sudden, what a delightful surprise he finds when he opens his briefcase and reaches for the notes he made to take into his morning meeting. Maybe you can add a sultry note, "Uh, honey. Yeah, it's me. Say, what are you doing for lunch?"

I cannot stress this enough, but don't even think you aren't sexy enough to star in this little fashion show. You are. Trust me. He won't see your self-perceived flaws through the lingerie. And for heaven's sake, don't point out or make profuse disclaimers to these flaws. This can only draw attention to them. Rest easy. If you don't bring them up, he probably won't notice them. I remember once when I was in a position that left my sun-aged arms a little less pleasant to look at. (Or at least they caught my attention.) I freaked out. I thought another person was beside me, and I almost stopped everything. When I heard from my man's lips just at the right time, "I love this little outfit you put on for me," it reminded me that men are just little sexual creatures who wear blinders when they are experiencing a sexual encounter. My arms were not even in his thoughts because my little outfit obviously clouded them. Thank God!

Let the Sex Games Begin

Remember being on the prowl? Well, it's fun at any age. You'll need a sexy dress, of course. Men love dresses on any woman, especially paired with some strappy heels. And while I'm on the subject, every woman deserves a new dress at least once every month or two. You may not feel you need one, but you do. Trust me on this.

I have heard this sentence a thousand times. Men will say, "I wish my wife would wear a dress like this one. It's so pretty, but she prefers the same-ol'-same-ol' (her favorite pair of jeans)." If it is a money situation and you feel guilty, then stop. You can find almost-new dresses at secondhand shops or garage sales if you have to. And you deserve it!

You want your man to see you as the pretty woman he married, not the housewife who looks housewifely. It does not have to be expensive, just something new that looks feminine on you. You can cut back on the brand of toothpaste, toilet paper, paper towels, or whatever it takes to get some extra money, but don't cut back on yourself. Your man will enjoy the sexy you will portray. If you don't believe me, the next time you are out for an evening date, see what catches his attention. If a woman is anywhere close, wearing a dress and heels, his eyes will be glued. Well, at least until you knock his head off. Oh, well! At least you can poke them out!

Still, as great as the dress is, what's underneath will blow his mind. Well maybe, that is if you don a pair of stockings and a garter belt. If this procedure is tantamount to rebuilding a car engine for you, any upscale lingerie shop will have an undies expert who can tutor you. This could be one of those rides to the restaurant or home that he won't soon forget. That's another good reason to wear a dress. So please, ladies, if you don't like to wear dresses, just try this experiment.

But for now, I can give you a few written basics:

- Put your stockings on first and then the garter belt. The panty should go on last for two reasons:

  - Should nature call, you won't have to undo and then redo the whole sexy rig.
  - As things heat up a little later, your man can pull them off without having to disturb the rest of the pretty picture you make in your sexy ensemble.

Remember, men are visual creatures, and you want to maintain that stocking fantasy mystique. Be warned that the sight is likely to drive him mad. He may spontaneously combust at the sight, especially if this is the first time you've ever donned such lingerie for him, so have the emergency numbers on hand. I know you have seen pinup girls on calendars from the twenties era. Some wore the stocking with the seam up the back of the leg (my husband's first choice). They were pretty risqué and very collectable now, especially if you find them in the original box.

- Now, if you can't bear the thought of wearing the stockings and garter duo (a pity, as this is a real treat for any man and you, too), use a sexy pair of thigh highs to achieve a similar effect. "Sexy" being the key word, girls. Or maybe the next time you climb into bed with your man, try wearing a pair of leather knee-high boots.

Lingerie Tip Reminder

Wear thigh highs with a wide band. The ideal width is three to four inches. They'll stay up, and best of all, they'll spare you that ghastly thigh bulge. For you ladies who feel you have less than perfect thighs, put on a garter belt and a pair of sexy stockings. Look for some with a Cuban heel and some with designs and patterns. It's a fail proof plan. With all the silky hosiery on, your guy will be too preoccupied to even notice any trouble spots. Now remember, as mentioned above, to put on your garter belt and stockings first and then your thongs or panties. That way, you can easily pull down your panties when you need a bathroom break and won't have to worry about unhooking your garter. Also when you are playing, you can discard the panties and still have on the stockings and garter. A sure way to really heat up the moment!

They can really make your legs look great and work wonders if you are one of those women with less than perfect legs. Not only do they hide the cellulite and any imperfections you may have, men really are such visual creatures that they see glamour when they see stockings. Trust me. I will tell you, ladies, that, in the winter months, not only are stockings very sexy to your man, it's a lot easier to go to the bathroom instead of those pantyhose that's hard to pull up and down, which I used to always put my fingernail through. In the dog days of summer, this would be a good time to wear stockings if the occasion calls for them instead of pantyhose. And they are so much cooler, especially on those hot summer nights. If you still are not convinced about wearing a pair of stockings or fishnets, then I highly recommend a fishnet body stocking. Not only will it cover any flaws you may have, it will make you look alluring and mysterious at the same time.

At this point, I shouldn't have to add (but I will) that high heels are a must. They're not called "fuck me pumps" for nothing, pardon my French.

Now, a few hours before, call your man and tell him to meet you at your favorite restaurant or any eatery with a romantic ambience and sexy atmosphere. (Good food is optional.) You should arrive early in order to procure a booth (dimly lit and secluded, naturally) and relax with a drink. Take a deep breath, and let your inhibitions fade away. Also ask your hostess if she can seat you at a booth assigned to a young and handsome waiter. You'll see why in a minute.

Now, don't be shocked. Think yourself into a sultry, sensual mood. Use these solitary moments to reflect on the past and all the amorous feelings you felt when you first knew him. Think of the tender and racy things you said to one another. Recall that sense of constant wondering you had and all the things you were curious about, like what it would be like to make love to and with him. Think of the raw edge of anticipation of the act and fulfillment it would bring. How about when you seduced him and/or he seduced you? Now, this is that time again.

It might sound terribly unromantic, but seduction often requires planning, especially as we get older or have been married for a long time. It sometimes takes much thought to make something appear thoughtless and spontaneous.

Now, clear your mind of everything but him.

"Yes, waiter, I'll have another . . . Good heavens! Who is that handsome man who just walked into the room? You simply must know! Wait! He's seen me!"

You bestow the look. You give the tilt. Oh, dear, your dress has slipped upward on your leg. He sees the top of your stockings peeping through. You pull your dress down, with a look of maidenly or virgin modesty. Not too much too soon. Just a taste.

He's coming near. You glance down suggestively at the seat beside you. He takes it. You wait for him to greet you first. You reply in the voice and ask what sort of cocktail he would like. Try emphasizing the first part of that word just a bit, and watch the spark in his eye. While he's ordering, cross and uncross your legs several times, drawing attention to them. He must recall the peeping stockings of the moment before. Trust me. He remembers them.

Be sure no one is looking. Don't worry too much about the waiter though. Catching his eye might be a good thing for your man to observe. All men secretly want to be with a woman that other men find desirable. My husband once caught the waiter smiling at me. He took hold of my chair and pulled it closer to his. I just smiled. I knew what I was doing, and it worked. It's one sure way to remind him not to take you for granted.

Take his hand, and rest it atop your knee or thigh for several moments. Then take it and move it up your leg so he can savor the feel of your stockings. Now that you've got him where you want him, employ the voice in a little dirty talk. Whisper "Like what you see?" into his ear as you lightly pinch his inner thigh and run your hand up his leg, stopping right before you reach his privates. Add seductively, "I hope so because this is just the appetizer."

Now that I've got you started, I'll leave you to your own imagination with the dirty talk. I have every confidence in you. Dirty talk is pretty idiot-proof. I mean, we are talking about men here. That is another reason why men love porn. And please, don't think that men don't love watching porn. Most men will tell you they don't, but they are like little boys in a candy store getting caught with their hands in the jar (or, in this case, in their pants).

The next time you and your man go out to dinner, leave your panties at home. After you've ordered and are waiting for your meal, drop your napkin or a fork, and ask your man to reach down and pick it up. Of course, you know what will be down there waiting for him to see, so make sure your legs are just a little spread.

If this sort of public seduction makes you uncomfortable, here's an option. You can always re-create this movie-like seduction scene at (or on) your own candlelit dining table. You can also move the setting outdoors to your patio, garden, or even cozy rug in front of the fireplace. Wherever you chose, just make sure it will be an evening he won't soon forget. Tease him like you use to tease your hair, a little stroke at a time, but make sure you put out in the end. Be his Marilyn Monroe, the sexy seductress of his dreams. Don't be shy. I know you can do it. We all have a little actress in us just waiting for our big chance.

Or if you don't choose to leave your panties at home, try this one. It will surely get him hot and bothered. After a couple drinks, get up and take a trip to the ladies room. When you come back to the table, shove your panties into his hand.

Then lean over and whisper into his ear, "I really am feeling a little frisky tonight!"

Let him watch you sip your cocktail as you slowly suck on your straw. When the food arrives, give him some small samplings of your food. Make sure you feed it to him. While you slowly slide that fork into his mouth, give him that sultry smile. Dessert? Yes, by all means! The finale to any evening! Order only one to share.

Tell him in the voice, "I don't usually share my dessert with just anyone." Let him watch you as you slowly put the spoon in your mouth, and then, with all the oomph in you, lick that spoon clean. Before you know it, dinner will be over, but the night will have just begun.

If you would rather give your man a night of erotic pleasure at home, put on nothing else but a pair of stockings (maybe a pair of fishnets) and lie him down anywhere on his back. With his legs closed, climb on to and straddle him with your back to him. Then slowly bend over until you are almost facing his feet. This will give him a good look at all your goodies. As you feel his excitement, bend over and raise your buttocks as high in the air as you can. Remember, men are very visual creatures. Sights like this really drive them wild. After he is fully erect, stand up, but don't turn around. Then slowly lower yourself down until your vagina is touching the top of his penis. Rotate yourself around on top of his penis until you know he is totally hot. Slowly slide down on his erect penis until you have all of it inside you. Once you have him totally inside of you, slide up and down slow and then fast and then soft and then hard. After a few minutes, bend forward as far as you can so he can see himself moving in and out of you. Watch his excitement grow!

Ever tried anal eroticism on your man? Well, maybe it's time! But whatever you do, don't ask him if he would like it. Most men believe that only homosexuals enjoy anal pleasure. After you have been enjoying foreplay for a while and he's fully excited, guide him on all fours while you position yourself behind him on your knees. Grab his hips with both your hands, and pretend you are humping him like a dog. After a few minutes, take your hands, and gently spread open his buttocks. Take one of your fingers (preferably one with the shortest nail) gently. Very slowly, slide that finger in and out of his anus. Once in a while, take your other hand and reach around and stroke his balls and penis. If he truly gets excited this time, you can make it a little more exciting by adding anal toys next time. Some actually have vibrating stimulators on them. Fun! Men seem to like the thought of anal sex, and women, turnabout is fair play.

Real-Life Story

Misty, another customer of mine, shared with me that once she brought an anal toy home and did not even show it to her husband. She just pulled it out and started rubbing it all over his body. When she felt he was the most excited, she just slid it in. She knew right away that she liked it; however, she said they have (not to this day) ever talked about it. She still pulls it out once in a while when she feels she needs to spice things up a little.

9

Ladies, Start His Engine

You are to follow the contents of this chapter with extreme caution. The writer does not assume any responsibility for the safety of any reader following these suggestions. Common sense and responsible driving are to be expected at all times. Drive at your own risk!

Remember one of the first books you read in elementary school? *See Dick and Jane. See Dick and Jane take a drive.* Sounds simple, doesn't it? It doesn't have to be. With the right twists (and right turns), a simple drive can be transformed into a delightfully complicated affair. How? *See Jane put on a pretty skirt.* See Jane not put on any panties!

Tell Dick you want to take a drive. The destination is not required. Let him drive you through an area where there is little traffic and few pedestrians. At some point, out of the blue, hike up your skirt but heed any "warning" signs, and be absolutely sure it's safe for him to look at that moment, when the car is temporarily motionless, for example. He'll never whine about a red light or stop sign again! After the skirt-hiking, open and close your legs slightly to tease him a little.

Say in the voice, "Look what I have for you!"

At the next stoplight, take his hand, and pull it inside your skirt. If the light is a long one (one can only hope!), tell him to slide his finger inside and "check the oil." When he does, moan a little. This will be his "green light" to accelerate (you, not the car). If you really want to drive him crazy (help, I can't stop the motoring puns!), take his finger (yes, that finger) and stick it in your mouth. Suck slowly. Pull out, and slide it back in again. Repeat as needed.

My husband and I once took a drive to the mountains to see the fall leaves. When we stopped at a red light, I don't know what hit me (maybe the fresh fall air), but I just got a little frisky. Before I knew it, I had hiked up my dress, grabbed his hand, and put it right up against my, well, you know. Then I started touching him everywhere. He smiled that sexy smile, and before I knew it, I was unzipping his pants. I think I will now let your imagination take it from here.

See Dick melt. See Dick swerve to avoid the streetlight. See Dick head for the nearest hotel. See Jane smile.

Real-Life Story

I had a really cute older couple who lived in Savannah that stopped by my boutique on their way to the Smoky Mountains in Tennessee. She told me it was so hot where they lived that she had talked "Paaaker" (how she pronounced her husband's name with a long Southern drawl) into taking her for a romantic drive for the weekend. "Peaches," as he called her, loved to wear pretty nighties so they looked online and decided my boutique was the most interesting. As Peaches looked around, she and I talked about lingerie, and she told me she always purchased a new nightie whenever they went on trips. She said Parker always told her how beautiful she looked, and it always seemed to put a smile on his face. That day, she chose a long, silky one. As I was ringing up the sale, they both were flirting with each other.

Parker said, "Well, Peaches, when are you going to wear this for me?"

She thought for a moment, and in her long Southern drawl, she said, "Well, Paaaker, I brought along a blanket and some mint julep, so maybe we could just stop along the roadside and find us a shady secluded spot. I might just try it on for you while you enjoy your drink!"

We all laughed. I'm sure she was just joking, but of course, I will never know. The teasing put a bigger smile on his face, and he grabbed her hiney.

"Peaches, you never seem to disappointment me, so let's get on the road!"

She smiled. "Paaker, you better slow down before you get us arrested."

He replied in his slow Southern drawl with his debonair Rhett Butler grin, "Frankly, my dear Peaches, I don't give a damn!"

I think the moral of this story is pretty lingerie mixed with a little teasing can keep a smile on your man's face, no matter the age.

A Little Lingerie Goes a Long Way

For some reason, women who feel their breasts are just not adequate enough to feel sexy in lingerie tend to shy away from wearing it. What a pity for your man if he desires to see you in such sexy underthings.

I was taught the following tip when I was training to measure breast size for bra fittings. Do not bend over from the waist and pull up your breasts to give you more cleavage. You are only stretching your breast tissue. The better way to obtain more cleavage is to stand with your feet shoulder width apart and stretch over to your right side with your left arm straight up, like when you were a little girl and bent from side to side as you sang "I'm a little teacup." When you can't bend anymore to your right, stop, take your right hand, grasp your left bra cup, and shake it until you feel all the meat of your left breast fall toward the middle of your chest. Repeat the steps on the other side using your left hand. When you stand up afterwards, you will see more cleavage than your grandma's method with less damage to your breast tissue.

I will tell you from years of experience that the best lingerie for small breasts is a bustier and one that has ruffles across the top. These ruffles are flirty and add inches as well. A customer once told me who was looking for something to make her small ("deflated beasts," as she called them) look perkier. She laughingly told me that she had perky breasts once, but her children had sucked the life out of them. So that is when I found out that putting her in a padded bustier not only added inches but also made her so-called deflated breasts a lot more perky. A teddy with an underwire or pads built in on the side of the cups is a sure way to give the illusion of larger breasts. Remember the saying that anything more than a mouthful is a waste? Men love small breasts just as much as large ones. It's like the size of a penis. It's what you do with what you've got that counts. Lingerie and the confidence you put on while wearing it will make any man happy. Remember, men are visual creatures. So, even if you feel self-conscious about the way certain parts of your body look or self-conscious about your breasts not being as perky as they once were, just remember lingerie. Or try this. Put on nothing but your favorite pretty robe, and add a pair of heels. Now ask him to unwrap you!

Real-Life Story

Once upon a time, a man came into my store in search of lingerie for his wife for an anniversary gift.

I asked, "What does she like to wear?"

He replied, "Mostly jogging suits or stretch pants and T-shirts and Granny panties."

He didn't really say granny panties, but he did say in a hesitant, sad voice that she did not like thongs or anything lacy.

He told me quietly, "I would love to see her wearing something more feminine and sexy although I understand why she doesn't want to." I asked him, "Have you ever told her how you feel?" "Yes," he replied, "on many occasions, but she feels fat and compelled to hide her body. I've often expressed to her how much I love her and I tell her I that her body is beautiful, but I can reassure you that it fell on deaf ears. I just think she doesn't really believe me."

I said "I think I would try to ease her into something at least soft and feminine. You should buy her what you want her to wear, keeping her feelings in mind."

I showed him a few things I thought would be appropriate. He settled on a pretty pink chemise that was not too revealing.

I said "Good choice! May I wrap it for you?"

He said "Yes" with a smile "and keep your fingers crossed for me," as he walked out the door, package in hand.

I assure you that this man is not alone in his frustration. He represents thousands of men in this same situation. Believe me. Over the past thirty years of owning a lingerie shop, I have heard it all.

What a pity! I would like to say to you women who are like this man's wife. Your body is the same under that big muumuu dress as it is under a sexy piece of lingerie. It would, however, feel nicer to his touch if what you were wearing were silk or satin, but I can assure you that, if your man still wants to have sex with you, then your body is not a problem. So give him the gift of something sexy on you. I believe it will give you an attitude adjustment if you just wear it.

Don't let your husband end up like this poor man. I know it may be hard at first, but give him what he wants, which is to see you. Trust me, sweetheart, if he loves you, you will please him. And wearing those god-awful granny panties is certainly not the way.

Start with something that is flattering but sexy. Sometimes, it doesn't take much. It really is as easy as simply changing your granny panties to something with a little lace. I personally love the Hanky Panky undies. Their logo says it all. "When it comes to style and comfort, we are behind you." They really are very comfortable. The lace is so soft, and the back is not the tight G-string that climbs up into your private parts. The lace is wide enough to stay in the proper place, and they make you feel really sexy the minute you put them on. Just try a pair. What do you have to lose? And you will certainly put a big smile on your man's face if he is used to only seeing you in those underwear your grandma wore. You don't have to wear them every day. If you just can't bear to wear them every day, you don't have to. That's okay. But, please, ladies, do wear them on special occasions for your man. Go ahead. Put a smile on his face. Isn't your relationship worth it?

If you still do not want to wear a thong and, no matter what I say, you have decided these pretty little things are just not for you, then I have a question for you. Does whatever panty you wear every day at least match your bra? This question most definitely should be answered with a great big YES!

Remember when your mother always told you to make sure your underwear was clean because you never know when you might have to be taken to the hospital and you sure would not want to be caught not wearing clean undies. Would you? Well, I'll take Mom's advice a step further. Not only is lingerie one of the easiest ways to make yourself feel pretty, it also gives the man in your life something to enjoy seeing when you dress in the morning or undress in the evening. Even if sex is not in the picture, then at least give your man a pretty picture to look at. Men do notice what you are wearing, especially when you take off your clothes for whatever the reason. Women seem to not think wearing matching undies is very important, but let me assure you. It is!

I was once in a very bad car wreck, and the ambulance attendant had to cut my dress off me to be able to attach the heart monitor to my chest. I have to admit that, not only do I love pretty lingerie, but I have never left my house without my panty matching my bra. Most of the time, my undies are the same color as the clothes I am wearing. My husband always tells me it is one of the one hundred and one reasons he married me. (I admit it is easier because I own a lingerie boutique.)

As the EMT cut from the bottom of my dress all the way up past my bra, he stopped and made an astonished sound. His face had a look of embarrassment as he very apologetically said, "I am so sorry. In all the years I have been doing this, I have never seen such pretty lingerie!" (They were iced mint green to match the dress I had on).

After I was taken to the hospital and before the EMT left, he came over to my bedside and apologized to me again. He then said he wished his wife would wear pretty matching undies like the ones I was wearing.

The point I am trying to make is, ladies, it is not that hard to pick out matching undies, and it is something so tiny and easy to do for your man. I bet your panties matched your bra when you were dating your man. Remember, men are very visual. Believe me. They do notice! My son happened to walk in when a nurse standing by heard the EMT and asked where I purchased these pretty undies. My son handed her a business card and then handed the EMT one. (What an drastic way to advertise our business!)

Remember, it is a small thing to do, but what a big impact it makes on your man. What a nice surprise you have just given him when he accidentally gets a peek at you when you both are getting dressed for work.

That visual scene he just saw will be in his mind during the day as his mind wanders away from that drenching morning meeting. Never forget that the other woman would never NOT wear matching panties and bras. I know because I sell them to women who are single much more than I do to married women. Sadly, more often than not, the married woman will say, "I just don't care if they match. I don't think he even notices anyway . . . I don't want to spend the extra money for the panty. I just need a bra."

So many times, I want to shout, "Good grief, lady. These panties aren't that expensive!"

Believe me. It will make such a difference in your mind while wearing pretty undies and in his when he accidentally gets a peek. We women seem to let things slide like that and use too many excuses, but trust me. You will be glad you did. I know I was when I had my car wreck. Please! They don't have to be expensive. They just need to match, and I don't mean WHITE!

Real-Life Story

A female customer recently came into my shop. She looked to be around fifty. After letting her browse a while, I asked her, "Is there anything I can help you with?"

She replied, "My husband gave me some money to buy new undies and told me that he was going to empty all my underwear into the trash while I was gone!"

I asked her, "What kind of undies do you like to wear?"

Not to my surprise she said, "Cotton and no thongs."

I showed her everything I thought she would like that was not cotton or granny panty, but after about twenty minutes, she left, saying she just felt more comfortable in cotton briefs. I could not help but feel sorry for the both of them because she seemed to lack self-confidence and he clearly was tired of seeing the same old getup on his wife. Ladies, maybe you can wear your granny panties and add some lace or a thong once in a while for him.

10

The Erotic Realm of the Senses

Over a millennium ago, a book was written in India called the *Kama Sutra of Vatsayayana: Aphorisms on Love.* You should definitely check it out. Kama Sutra takes you back to very ancient times to India, where sexuality was an integral part of life and an avenue to spiritual bliss.

It is an ancient Indian text on human sexual behavior wildly considered to be the standard work on love in the Sanskrit literature. The author is believed to have lived between the first and sixth centuries AD, probably during the Gupta period. Naturally, it was a runaway bestseller. The images, with names like "Fairies in a Garden of Eden," make this book one you will want to read and reread.

Apart from the so obvious graphic illustrations of various sexual positions and wise advice pertaining to the act, this ancient tome also speaks of the existence of rare oils, exotic fragrances, and soothing unguents that undergird and enhance the sexual act and experience. Thus it was that Kama, the Indian god of love and sexual desire, inspired a line of massage oils, body lotions, and bath salts named Kama Sutra. It's magical.

Now, while I don't claim, as the book itself does, that the use of such concoctions possesses the power to bring lovers so close together that "flesh gleams in a shimmering pool of moonfire," I am quite confident that they are just the thing to usher you into the erotic realm of the senses with their subtly provocative physical sensations/magic. These products, which are 100 percent natural, are designed for one thing, to bring you and your lover closer and to encourage you to touch and perceive one another in a tenderly erotic way.

Many lingerie boutiques carry the Kama Sutra line. You can definitely find a selection of these sensory titillators at Karen's Beautiful Things. Don't forget to get a copy of the Kama Sutra itself to increase your general knowledge of sex. Men not wanting to read books that don't have pictures may enjoy this book and many others on Kama Sutra with all their graphics and illustrations.

"But how do I use them, Karen?" you ask.

Fear not, my young apprentice. Although it should be pretty obvious to you while reading the Kama Sutra, I'll try to give you a nudge in the right direction. You should definitely use these products before giving or receiving a massage. First, run a warm bath for two with "Treasures of the Sea" bath salts. Not only will these soften and clean the body, they'll make the moist air fragrant with tropical freshness. Your bathwater will be such a tranquil, beautiful aqua color that you'll think you are floating in the serene waters of an idyllic Caribbean sea. Not only will this bathing experience afford mental and physical relaxation and refreshment to the bathers, it can be a memorable form of foreplay. Not only can you soak your way into tranquility, it's a fun way to make sure all the inner parts of you and your man are fresh and clean.

Maintain the mood and continue the play by making drying off a cooperative venture. Armed with a fluffy towel, pat one another's body dry ever so gently. Don't rub. You want to maintain the moisture you've just pampered your skin with. Feel free to be creative. Pat the behind a little, and linger over the breasts. And don't forget the private areas. This could be a place you may want to dry off a little longer.

At this point, you may already want to make a beeline for the bed. Don't. Change your bedroom first into a tranquil boudoir. Make yourself a soft pallet. A fully opened sleeping bag makes a good base for this. Cover it with a soft sheet. I hope you don't need me to tell you this by now, Mary Lou, but do not . . . repeat, do NOT . . . use that old, ratty sheet your mother passed along when you got your first apartment. You know the one with the faded eighties-style blue and mauve country heart pattern all over it. Instead, use sheets and coverings pleasing to the eye. Something exotic looking is certainly apropos, preferably in silk or satin. These linens will visually compliment the pleasing fragrances you're about to savor. Now finish adorning your little love nest with some cushions and soft throw pillows for your head (and any other body parts you think you may be elevating). Again, granny panties are strictly verboten.

Put on some pretty feminine lingerie, preferably a long, sensuous gown. This is one time that sex should not be a factor in the lingerie choice. It should be time for romance. Add some strands of pearls, and don't forget a splash of his favorite perfume. Be his Cleopatra. Maybe he'll be your Caesar.

Now it is very important to make your bedroom into a very romantic and inviting space for the two of you. Make it the mood room. Try the following and see what a dramatic difference it will make. Combine silhouettes on the walls with flickering lights from lit scented candles and small, soft boudoir lamps. This will infuse the room with a serene, golden glow. Play some soothing, non-vocal music to set the mood and lend otherworldly ambience to the experience. Or, if you prefer, use calming nature sounds, like cooing doves or ocean waves breaking on shore. There are CDs available for purchase, like the ones used in a nice, reputable massage salon.

At the risk of repeating myself, as with any worthwhile endeavor, creating this experience may require a little prior thought and preparation. Fishing around in the utility room for candles while you're trying to get romantic may kill the mood.

When you and your man are all comfortable and relaxed, start with feeding him dessert in bed. Place a bed tray with legs in the

71

middle of the bed. Arrange his favorite undies on the bed beside the tray, just to let him know you are not wearing any panties. Be seductive. Your tray should be filled with edible items like strawberry whipped cream, cherry body butter, and some chocolate or vanilla warming massage oils. Then, make his fantasies come true!

At this point in the exercise, another Kama Sutra product I can wholeheartedly recommend is Honey Dust. And yes, its function is as enchanting as its name. It's a fine, silky smooth, and oh-so-kissable body powder. Better yet, it comes with a heavenly handmade feather applicator that will delight every nerve and sense under the skin to delight the dermis. Its operation is quite simple. Dip the feathers in the applicator, and trace your lover's body with it. The feathers will tingle, titillate, and arouse. It is edible and sugar free. Plus, it can make his private parts smell really yummy.

But don't have sex yet. Trust me. Deferred gratification can be all the better for your unhurried methods. Something tells me that you probably won't even make it to the bed.

If you are not into powder, may I suggest another sensual move you can put on your man or he on you. The Oil of Love is kissable, silky smooth, water-based oil. Use this during foreplay to intensify sensations and prolong pleasure. Apply all over the body, including erogenous zones. Activated by the warm breath of soft, intimate kisses, not only does this oil warm the skin, it can give you both soothing massages that relaxes and titillates you just by gently rubbing it on, along with leaving your skin tasting delicious for the intense lovemaking session you are about to enjoy without the unpleasant taste that perfume can leave.

A whole list of Kama Sutra products is available on the market. These are just a few of my favorite things.

Aphrodisiacs have been around for centuries. I've tried the following recipe, and it seemed to work for me. This recipe is made from all-natural ingredients. I, however, am not a doctor. If your doctor has prescribed a diet for you or put you on any medications, I suggest you follow your doctor's instructions. Now realize it is not my fault if this does not work for you. (You may need to try a couple shots of tequila or a bowl of steamed oysters!)

The Honeymoon Picker-Upper

This is an updated recipe of an ancient Druid formula. Sex therapists who prescribed it believed that taking it on a regular basis can generate a hearty sexual appetite.
Ingredients

- 2 level tablespoons of skim milk powder and water (according to the skim milk instructions)
- 1/4 teaspoon of powdered ginger
- 1/8 teaspoon of powdered cinnamon
- 2 tablespoons of raw honey
- A dash of lemon juice plus any fresh fruit or pure juice you care to add. Mix the above ingredients in a blender for several seconds. Blend and pour into a glass. Garnish with a slice of your favorite fruit on a cocktail pick. It's a great drink to have before the games begin.

Recipe for Edible Fun with Whipped Cream

Ingredients

- 1 pint heavy whipping cream
- 1-2 tablespoons confectioner sugar
- 1 teaspoon vanilla extract

Place two metal beaters in a large (glass) bowl in a refrigerator for at least four hours. Pour all or two-thirds of carton in bowl. Beat back and forth until it starts getting a little firm, about eight to ten minutes. Then add a cup of sugar and vanilla. Whip just a little longer, but no more than one-and-a-half minutes. If beaten too long, it turns to butter. Chill in the fridge. Enjoy!

11

Be a Prick Tease or the Appetizer

Y ou've all heard the term "prick tease" before. No? Sure you have. Maybe it's not what you want to be known for, except possibly by your lover or husband. Growing up during my school years, the girl known as a prick tease was not the girl you wanted to hang out with, but she sure was the girl who got all the boys' attention.

Once again, let us mentally traverse the boundaries of time and think about when you and your man were first dating. More specifically, recall the first time you both wanted sex (let's see . . . mmmm . . . that would have been with the dinner salad) but decided (at least YOU did) that it was too early in the relationship to succumb to physical passion.

"No, not yet," you said.

"No relationship should be based on sex" was the mantra that your mother and your more clear headed girlfriends repeated in your ear. Or perhaps you had already learned this lesson for yourself the hard way. So you did your damndest with the help of cold showers, girls' nights out, and a wide assortment of alternative sensual pleasures (bubble baths, chocolate, booze, and not to mention a good vibrator) to ease the deferment of sex until the relationship was well established on firmer foundations like trust, shared goals, mutual respect, a deeper understanding of one another's needs, and so forth. These same characteristics actually establish the ideal foundation of good sex anyway. So you were right to wait.

That said, despite your good intentions and wise deferment of sexual gratification, wasn't it beastly hard to keep your legs together, especially when the petting got heavy? Believe me. I've been there. I think we all have at least once.

Nonetheless, prudence is not always prudish. From a strictly sexual viewpoint, as hard as it was for your sexual appetite to wait, that waiting had the glorious benefit of increasing your lover's anticipation, desire, and lust. Denial whets the appetite. Oh, what a glorious feeling that was! Even the agony of longing can be strangely pleasurable and the suspense of unfulfilled ecstasy. Now is the time to recapture that intense passion. What's the secret? Here it comes! Are you *ready*? (It's a damn good one.) You're going to *love* it. Are you *sure* you're ready? Here it is!

Become a prick tease (huge emphasis on "tease"). Because Webster probably doesn't list this quaint little term in his dictionary (no, don't bother looking it up), I'll have to define it for you myself. A "prick tease" is a woman who promises the whole sexual world but delivers only a few acres at a time. She is one who engages in the practice of prick teasing.

How'd I do? Envision her as a slinky, sultry belly dancer. She promises and then says no. She offers and then denies. She moves forward and then withdraws. Let your whole body gaze in manner as if to say yes, but your answer must be no. (This is not your final answer, of course. That would just make you cruel.)

This prick tease "dance" will help keep his appetite sharp and his desire hot and bothered. It's just one simple principle, not magic. Men want what they can't have. If you deny him you in the right way, he'll want nothing more than to have you. Give him just enough for the moment and no more. For years, men have gone to burlesque shows, and now they seek the Las Vegas shows to see the almost naked girls dance. So now it's your turn. Dance for your man, damnit!

Here's one version of the dance. Make it a game. Tell him that he'll get a reward if he's a good boy. Let him touch your breast through your blouse, but don't let him inside. Just moan a little. Slide his hands on your backside for a little squeeze while giving him a little kiss, maybe with a little tongue. **Note of caution:** Don't touch him too intimately yet. Remember, you are a tease.

Tell him to stick out his tongue, or gently coax it out with your own. Gently suck on it. It'll drive him wild, not that you need me to tell you that. Did we not learn in our younger days that a man loves to have a woman suck his tongue (their anything really)? I know you know that men love to have their fingers sucked as well.

After a few minutes, begin caressing him ever so subtly in his private areas. At this point, he's earned first base, so let the poor man have it. Gently brush against him, and pull or pinch his nipples. Yes, men like that!

Just keep your legs together until you're ready. Keep saying no, and put up a stern resistance, torturing him with his own desire. *Gradually*, allow him to break down your barriers of refusal. (Yes, we know you're a "sure thing" here. The trick is to convince him otherwise.) Remember, men love to be in ultimate control, especially in the bedroom. They love to envision themselves as seducer (Valentino, lover irresistible) or conqueror (Attila, barbarian ravisher). By not immediately satisfying his moment-to-moment wants, you'll frustrate his need, and he will want you even more. You may even have him begging. (Pssst! Now's the time to ask for diamonds.)

The prick tease dance can be as long and drawn out as you like. Remember, nice girls don't say yes until they just can't say no anymore.

Remember that other quaint phrase, "dry humping," an expression typically associated with the good old date night at the drive-in. (What *was* that movie?) Well, it's not just for the teenager and desperate virgin anymore. It's a great way to tease and torture (the delightful kind) your lover. Those were the nights when the heavy petting felt so good that you forgot to say no, and before you knew it, you were letting him push your clothes and panties aside to touch you there in your forbidden place. Fast-forward to the present, and pretend you're back in the car with your man. A good dry hump will take him back to his own drive-in days and the frenzied sexual escapades that fogged up his Chevy windows.

Okay, let's review the prick tease steps. Tease and then refuse. Promise and then deny. Resist and then surrender . . . little by little.

Maybe the next time you are out having dinner with your man, see if you can spot a single woman out with her date. She will be the one teasing her man with that sheepish grin and tilt of the head and probably squeezing her man's leg. She's giving him the sexual look. So watch. You may pick up some invaluable techniques.

Call Me! Phone Sex

When you don't have time for sex, consider phone sex on your lunch hour (sure beats the usual boring diet!) Just call him up and say things you would not normally say or things you would like to say in the bedroom but are afraid to say. You'll be surprised how easy this comes over the phone. Don't let your hang-ups get in the way. Just pretend you're getting paid a lot of money like a sex operator. There are phone books or online sites that give good instruction on the art of phone sex. You can find one most likely at any adult store, but I bet, if you tried hard enough and let your inhibitions go, you could do it all on your own. Maybe the next time your husband calls on his way home from work to let you know there has been an accident and he is stuck in traffic, you can help his stress level by talking a little dirty to him. This can create a fantasy he can remember for later or a jump-start for the both of you when he gets home.

When I was a flight attendant, I was gone sometimes on a four-day trip. My husband would call me on the phone at night just before I went to bed, and we would talk for hours. Sometimes, our conversations led to sexual ones, and I have to admit they were the best and exciting phone conversations I'd ever had. We still to this day talk about some of the conversations we had. If your husband or partner travels on overnight trips, this might be a way to keep him in his room at night. Don't be a prude. It is also a great way to masturbate with each other and a fun way to keep in touch. (Pardon the pun!) These days, with all the gadgets and cell phone apps, you can do a lot of sexy things for your man. Try sending him a kiss or sexy picture of yourself via his cell phone, or you can sex text him. This can be a fun little adventure for the both of you if you keep your mind open!

12

Get out of Your Box

The most delightful pleasures cloy without variety.
Publilius Syrus
Sameness is the mother of disgust, variety the cure.
Petrarch

Do you set sexual limitations on yourself? Or on your man? Has sex become repetitive and predictable? Are you too shy, conservative, distracted, or just plain chicken to be creative in the bedroom, kitchen, closet, bathroom, and so forth?

There's only one cure for it. Take a risk. What do you have to lose? I can tell you honestly that you have everything to gain. Maybe you can put on a wig once in a while. If your hair is short, get a long wig. If your natural hair is brunette, get a blonde wig. Change can be fun for you as well as something different for him. A customer told me that she buys several colors and styles of wigs because she is Jewish with very dark hair and very conservative because of her religion. She said she loves to role-play and does not care if her husband pretends she is another woman. She just wants to keep their sex life fun, and she has really enjoyed playing the part of a blonde slut the most.

"I just put on my highest strappy heels and a short, slutty dress. I meet my husband at the door as he arrives home from work," she said, beaming.

We both laughed as I jokingly called her a trollop!

Risk taking in the bedroom can jump-start a dull relationship or freshen a stale love affair. One should never get too comfortable physically with one's partner. Don't be like that old but comfortable pair of shoes you don't want to throw away.

Still, if you're having a hard time climbing out of your sexual comfort box, just take things slow at first. Start with a simple story. Everyone loves a story, right? Well, this will be a story about you and your desires.

Still having a hard time getting started? Close your eyes. Delve deep into the recesses of your imagination, and take hold of your most secret erotic fantasy, the one you won't even tell your best friend.

Got it? Good. Remember, this is your story. It can be a fantasy about anything or anyone within reason. Just remember, erotic, not gross. Don't get perverted. Just have fun with it. You don't want to do anything that could get you arrested. Sex with a stranger is a good one to start with. Or how about having sex under the tree in the backyard? (Please respect the neighbors.) A seduction can be in a public place, like a woman's restroom in a movie theater or a ladies' room of an elegant restaurant. There is always the usual sex on a blanket on the beach taken by surprise by drinking too many piña coladas. You could pretend you just met him at the tiki hut, and after a few cocktails, take hold of his hand, take a walk into the ocean, and have your way with him. Or maybe in the treehouse you built for your kids! Just make sure that you're wise with your fantasies. Some fantasies should stay just that, a fantasy.

Have your favorite cocktail or two. Write down your fantasy. Make sure it is written on a pretty note pad, and whisper it in his ear with as much detail as you can come up with. Your story will give him a memory to carry in the back of his mind. Tell him the story on your birthday, and he'll never forget the date again. If you find yourself without a fantasy of your own, feel free to borrow one. There's no copyright.

Now, there is one fantasy that most, dare we say all, men have at some point in their life. Some men even talk to their buddies about this fantasy, namely, girl-on-girl intimacy. Now, no one is suggesting that you must take this fantasy to its fullest realization, of course. (There is risk involved that can create another set of problems, the very kind we are trying to avoid.) I'm suggesting that fantasies are very powerful in and of themselves. That is, the mere idea of you kissing another girl might suffice to spark his imagination and heighten his desire, especially if you mention to him that you might like to do it one day. At this point, he's already envisioning it. I assure you. Remember when Madonna kissed Britney Spears on stage? People talked about that kiss for months. (I know my husband loves the song "I kissed a girl and I liked it" by Katie Perry). Sometimes, I sing it just to tease him!

There are girl-on-girl movies. Might I suggest you check them out. Maybe one evening, you and your man could watch a girl-on-girl adult movie. Some are very erotic. Look for some that feature Jena Jamison and Amber Lynn. They are two famous porn stars. I will warn you jealous ladies in advance that both these women are sexy and beautiful but their movies at least have a story line to them and they are somewhat tastefully done. To take the edge off and get more relaxed, pour yourself a glass of wine, light some incense, and grab some massage oil.

Real-Life Story

One of my customers related an encounter she and her husband had on a vacation to Jamaica. They ventured on to the hedonism beach in Jamaica where nearly everyone was partially or totally nude. After one too many strawberry daiquiris, the two struck up a conversation with another couple sitting nearby. As one thing led to another, they all ended up relaxing in a hot tub. There, the conversation took a titillating turn.

The subject? Girl-on-girl sex. At some point, the two girls decided between them to give their husbands a rare and tantalizing peep show by bringing this common male fantasy to life. It involved a little kissing and caressing of one another's breasts as well as a little rubbing up against each other. I'm sure the thermostat in that hot tub was close to exploding!

My customer related that, after a few more drinks, she and her husband went back to their room and had the best sex ever. After ten years, they still love to talk about the experience. He still calls her Tina (the name he uses when he wants to role-play) when he wants to experience the fantasy. Or when she wants to get her groove on and jump-start the evening, she tells her husband, "Tina is here in the house tonight!"

Of course, I'm not saying you should have a fantasy in real life. That can be dangerous. The whole objective here is to get other women out of his mind. All I'm saying is that talking about taboo sexual subjects and nibbling at the edges of experimentation can be very sexually stimulating, both mentally and physically. Such experiences, planned or spontaneous, may make your lover see you in an entirely new way. In short, keep yourself unpredictable, "not housewifely."

Real-Life Story

A never-married customer, Ginger, always enters a room with a sexy "sit, walk, and talk" about her. She is constantly checking herself out in the nearest mirror for any flaws. Ginger is not what you call beautiful. (So, you ladies out there who think you can't flirt because you don't feel beautiful, take note.) She just portrays beautiful with the confidence she has, and I do believe that men find her beautiful. She loves to wear sexy dresses and drive men wild with the flirting that seems to come natural to her. She once told me that she has never married because she feels men never ever stay true and they always have a hunger for what they can't have. She once revealed to me that she mostly dated married men.

Seeing my shocked expression, she explained that this was not by choice. She had always wanted to get married, but the right man had just not come along. She, however, does date single men, but it seems the married ones are the ones who come on to her more. She said these men, for the most part, don't want to leave their wives but stray chiefly because they aren't getting much sex. Either that or the excitement of the act is gone. For herself, she is past longing for marriage, and in her view, however misguided, such relationships present a convenient arrangement for her.

Her actions with men probably tainted her finding her own Prince Charming. She gets what she wants (sex); they get what they want (sexual thrills) without burdening her with the upkeep of a man. I cite this example, not as justification for adultery, but as a friendly warning.

Ginger uses this technique also to make herself keep in shape. She works out daily and has had several cosmetic procedures. I have to admit she sure looks great for her age. She could definitely pass for at least ten years younger than someone in her fifties. She is a very animated woman and very sensual. I do not in any way condone what Ginger does, but she needs something, he needs something, and she feels she is helping the wife in the long run because it's not ever long term and she does not want to take him away. It's only in their fantasies! This is why the term "the other woman" was born.

Unless you're not disturbed at the idea of your man getting his real pleasure/sexual thrills with someone else, please consider trying a little novelty/variety/adventure in the bedroom. You might just awaken your own senses. Wouldn't that just be too perfect?

It doesn't take a snooty Manhattan chef to know that, if you make a salad the same way every time with the same veggies, same dressing, and same bowl, you'll soon tire of eating salad. Yet a few simple changes can make a surprising difference. You may find that serving your salad in a crystal parfait glass with a sterling fork (that you otherwise never use) and dining on the living room floor by candlelight will make consuming the same salad a little more interesting.

Just so, exercise your creative imagination in the bedroom like you would in the kitchen. Serve up something new; add a little more spices. Experiment with different recipes. Stimulate his appetite for you with some novelty and variety. Bon appétit!

Afraid to Try New Things?

Are you afraid to try new things for fear of looking silly? Well, throw out those old-fashioned hang-ups. Sex can be a thrilling, fun, and positive adventure. So don't be shy of taking a walk on the wild side. (Yes, you have one). We all do. We just don't want to admit it.

Real-Life Story

Fanny came into my shop, specifically to purchase a leather paddle. Feeling a compulsion to tell me exactly why she was buying such an item, she explained that she intended to play a little sex game with her husband. She had recently spent too much money on a new dress and was worried her husband would be angry at her purchase. To ameliorate his anxiety and distress and have a heck of a good time doing it, she decided to create the following scenario. She planned to take her husband into their den, sit him down, and penitently explain that she had been a very bad girl. Because she had been naughty, she confessed she deserved to have a spanking. At this point, amidst his shock, she decided to confess that she'd purchased a terribly expensive dress, pulled out her paddle, and told him to give her that spanking. Later, she planned to tell him that the dress purchase was a true story, but by that time, after the hottest sex they'd had in a while following the spanking he gave her, she doubted he'd be all that mad about it. She just hid it away in her closet and would tell him (like some of us do) that she had purchased it a long time ago.

This is just one scenario. With a little imagination, you can create your own. Don't let your man even think the grass is greener anywhere but right where he is!

And while we're on the subject of light spanking, it has the added benefit of increasing blood flow to the skin's surface and thereby increasing your body's sensitivity. So, if you find you like this sort of harmless disciplinary sport, try lifting your behind and allowing other places to be spanked lightly. If he gets a little carried away, a quick rub to the area will soothe the sting. A tip from another customer: use an aromatic and soothing lotion to ease any lingering tenderness.

Yes, my customers really do tell me, to my amazement, a little too much information!

13

Pole Dancing (Yes, I'm Talking to You)

F ew men will turn down the chance to see female legs wrapped around a pole, especially when those legs are attached to a scantily clad woman. (They're not picky about the pole.) That's where you and a pole come in. You've tried the waltz. You've done the tango. You did, heaven help us, the electric slide. Why not take a crack at pole dancing? It's a great way to lose weight and keep your body toned. Got your attention now?

"Where to begin?" you ask.

Well, first you need the right equipment. To that end, muster up your courage, and seek out your local adult store. Even some lingerie shops might just have what you need. There, you can most likely not only purchase the pole but also an instructional CD on how to do a pole dance for your man.

Real-Life Story

Several years ago, one of my customers approached me about ordering a pole for her. I called the rep of a company I order lotions and potions from, and sure enough, they did sell them, so I placed the order. When it arrived, I called the customer. She was so elated that she was there to purchase it, along with a few pieces of my risqué lingerie, within twenty minutes. As I rang up the sale, I teased her about what she was going to do with it. She explained to me that she had heard pole dancing was a great way to help keep you in shape in a more fun way so she wanted to give it a try.

Because I was now approaching my sixties and adamant about working out and keeping in shape, of course, I became inquisitive about how I could also learn to pole dance. She told me that, since she had become a personal trainer, she met another instructor who teaches any kind of dance you would ever want to learn, along with pole dancing.

I decided that this just might be a good way to have some fun with my customers. So, with some help from my customer and the dance instructor she introduced me to, we arranged to have a girls' night out party. I sent out invites to only my female customers who had purchased lingerie, lotions, and potions from me. The invite basically said, "You are invited to a *Girls Just Want to Have Fun* night. Bring a girlfriend or two but no boys allowed!" I also instructed them to bring along a comfy pillow as we would be sitting on the floor in the lingerie (or what I call the exotic room) area for a little pillow talk about erotica. I told them we were also having a lingerie fashion show followed by guidance on getting in shape by pole dancing and teasing their man at the same time.

To my surprise, we had so many girls show up that we hardly had the floor space to accommodate them. As most girls had not met each other before, they were reluctant to open up and converse about their sex life. But after I poured them all a glass of wine, let's just say that we got the party started. We talked about everything under the sun and the moon. Then when it came time to climb the pole, they again got a little apprehensive, so I poured them another glass of wine. Magically, their inhibitions disappeared. I can honestly say that we had the most fun trying to dance around and climb that pole that the girls did not want the party to end. Finally, around eleven o'clock, the dance instructor had to go, so with no further ado, we wrapped the evening up, that is, after we unwrapped the legs of a customer who was just having too much fun.

While my customer helped me clean up, we started talking and laughing about how a little wine made all of us open up and enjoy the evening. My customer then shared her little secret with me. Because she had paid close to two hundred dollars for the pole, she told me she wanted to maximize her investment by utilizing her newfound skill to excite her man. And yes, he even puts money in her G-string. Lots and lots of extra spending money! She also shared with me that she invented herself a stage name, "Kashmere." So when she climbs atop that pole, she really becomes Kashmere, the sexy exotic dancer for her man.

Kashmere told me she always makes sure her lingerie chest is full of new sexy costumes, which she of course buys from Karen's Beautiful Things. She told me her man's very favorite was the black lace garter belt and G-string with the matching demi bra she first purchased from me. And she never forgets to strap on her six-inch stiletto heels. She also always makes sure her lips and nails are painted a streetwalker's red.

Kashmere also revealed to me that, on occasion, she will call her man on the phone and talk sultry to him. She says she loves to tantalize him by telling him Kashmere is waiting to be his naughty stripper. She will meet him at the door in one of her costumes, hand him his favorite cocktail, and escort him to his VIP seat. Then as he sips his drink, she dances around his chair and ends her escapade with a gyrating and grinding sexy lap dance. She says she believes this pleasurable show keeps him happy and content because he never frequents strip clubs.

I just laughed and replied, "I can't even imagine why he would ever need to!"

All I can say is she must really do a number on that pole because she is one of my best customers!

Real-Life Story

I do have strippers who come into my boutique for lingerie and lots and lots of stockings. (I guess they don't last too long.) They usually leave me with a story or two. Candie shared that her best paying customers were married men. They usually tell their wives they are in an after-work meeting and head out to the strip club to see her dance. She sure must make a lot of money because everything she buys is with cash, and I mean a lot of cash! I wonder sometimes why men pay her so much money because honestly she really is not that attractive, but then again, she thinks she is. A lesson learned from her: being pretty is not required.

If you don't want to erect (pardon the pun) poles in your house because, after all, they can be hard to hide, substitute a chair with no arms. Arrange the furniture to suit your dance, and afford adequate space for movement. You never know how much room you will need once you start strutting your stuff.

Now sex yourself up. Put on something sexy and, of course, easy to remove. If you have no feminine, sexy clothes, visit your local boutique immediately. All ladies should invest in some sexy outfits. If you lack the wherewithal, temporal or financial, to go out and shop for an elaborate new outfit, just make a quick visit to a lingerie shop and purchase a pair of fishnet stockings and garter belt. Trust me. They'll have them. If they don't, never darken the door of that establishment again. This age-old duo can be paired with anything or nothing at all to achieve a similar effect.

Of course, you mustn't forget the heels! Men go nuts over stockings and heels. The higher, the better. Strappy ones are a real turn-on. (Remember Kashmere!) And unless your man has a particular fetish for bare feet, these are a top priority. Just be careful in your sexy shoes as you dance around so you don't injure yourself. That goes double for pole dancing.

Pole dancing not your thing? Another option is to surprise him by strutting onstage in one of his Oxford dress shirts. Men love to see women wearing their shirts after sex. You know, the kind perfectly designed for slow, gradual unbuttoning, like in the movies when you see the woman wearing the man's shirt after they have just had a hot, steamy sex scene. Now, start with a flash of your leg. As you dance, you'll undo these buttons one by one. This can be done in slow sequence or intermittently with a little dance in between. This forces him to wait for the next button to come free and expose just a little more skin. His passion will *grow* as he counts them down one at a time.

To further accentuate the pole dance or what-have-you experience, set the mood with some good tunes carrying a sexy beat, with maybe even some suggestive lyrics. Start with a strut or two round the chair. Then sit in it, kick up your legs, and then turn and straddle the seat. Laugh at him as he falls off his own. If you don't want to take all your clothes off, of course, that's okay. You can stop at any point you feel most comfortable. Who knows? Perhaps this little titillating and tantalizing act will get you so excited yourself that you will want to jump right off that chair and onto his lap. I do promise you, however, that, if you do decide to take all your clothes off in a very slow, gyrating dance, he will only notice the excitement in his pants, not any of your flaws, especially not the ones only you see.

I used to feel pretty self-conscious when I first tried to dance for my man, but you just have to muster up the courage and just do it, or so I was told. I did. I have to admit that he loved it, and I really had a fun time doing it.

One of my favorite songs to get me into "tease dancing" is the one by Melissa Etheridge, "I'm the Only One." Another is an old song, "Black Velvet" by Alannah Myles. They both seem to have that slow, gyrating beat. If I add my favorite cocktail while I get dressed for the part, then I'm ready to give my man a show. You just have to pick a song that will make you want to get up and strut your stuff.

By now, having watched his excitement and whatever else swell, you'll have gained more confidence (unless you never needed it to begin with). Now you can more easily continue with the dance, improvising your own moves and positions and feeling the music.

Experiment with different kinds of eye contact as you dance. Sexy, innocent, and even a little haughty will certainly get his attention. Just make sure you give him that sultry-come-hither look. Don't forget to turn your hiney toward him and bend over once or twice, like you were touching your toes. Men love the back entrance fantasy, so go on. At least tease him with it. Watch how he responds to each. Not only will it boost your confidence even further, it will also help you know what thrills him the most. Let your own eyes gaze up and down his body. Lick your lips sensuously. Now would also be a good time to talk a little dirty talk, that is, let him know what is in store for him.

Don't worry about looking silly. Trust me. Your movements and eye contact will most likely hypnotize him and get him so riled up that he won't know if he is coming or going. Dating back to the Arabian nights, even the sheiks had harems. They sat for hours watching their harem girls dance and grind for them. Believe me. Men from every century have had a weak spot for dancing girls. Your man will be unable to resist you. Trust me on this one. Have you ever seen a man walk out of a room when there are naked women in there . . . and dancing naked women at that? I can tell you with complete confidence that the answer is a definitive no. So just get your sexy on and give him a show he won't soon forget. I promise you won't look silly at all.

14

Role-Playing and Fantasies

I have talked a little about role-playing already, but I thought I would take the time to really discuss this type of erotic play date. Want to really make your man glad he didn't stop off with the guys before coming home after work?

Greet him at the door with a French maid outfit on, and tell him you are serving dessert for dinner. Have a bottle or two of edible (different-flavored) massage oil. Take him into the bedroom, rub the oil all over him, and just let him enjoy you licking it off. You can put on a leather teddy and some leather boots. If you grab a leather whip, you'll have him down on his knees. I'm sure you know where I am trying to go with all this, and if you dare to, "Get your domination on!" Be in control, and tell him what to do.

If you really want to spice things up, play the part with props, if needed, of his fantasy, and make it as real as you can. Wear a costume that you think your man will like.

A customer told me she dressed up as the ever-appealing French maid. So garbed in her uniform and a feather duster in hand, she met her husband at the door, took off his clothes, and dusted his entire body with edible dust. Now when she dresses up he calls her "Fifi."

If you don't find a feather duster appealing, try a small can of Kama Sutra dusting powder. It's edible and comes with a sexy feather applicator. If you're no French maid, try the naughty nurse. You can put him in the bed as you give him his meds. Men sometimes act like babies when they are sick, so this costume is sure to make a grown man cry. A few other suggestions are fairy princess (grant him three wishes) or the sultry harem girl (do a little naughty dance for him). How about a Playboy bunny? Serve him his favorite cocktail while you wiggle your tail at him. Whichever you choose, lingerie shops do have full dress-up costumes. You can even special order them at some lingerie shops.

Another customer related her experience to me recently. She played the role of the winsomely innocent Catholic schoolgirl, complete with plaid miniskirt, lacy ankle socks, a pair of heels, and pigtails. When she revealed herself in all her parochial glory, her man was so excited, as was she, that she could hardly keep him from spanking her for skipping school. The only role I might not suggest to you is playing his secretary. If he has one already, you certainly don't want to put any ideas in his head. However, if he does not have one, then, by all means, put on a sexy tight shirt with a blouse not fully buttoned. Don't forget the glasses and heels. Then jump onto the nearest desk with pen in hand and ask him to "dicktate" to you.

You can get a pair of soft, furry handcuffs, but only if you are into role-playing. This is a fun fantasy for your sensuous, naughty endeavors or when you want him to see things your way. Just cuff him to the bed and straddle him until he gives in. You can tease him and promise a reward if he agrees with all your demands. Let your imagination work in your favor here. Just a little tip, you will need two pairs if you are using the bedposts.

I promise you, ladies, men really love to play out their fantasies. First, find out what fantasy your man has. Then pick a night and just do it. Even if you don't think you could be the one in his fantasy, you will be pleasantly surprised.

Help! There's a Strange Man in My Fantasies!

Have you ever had a fantasy about sex with another man? I mean while you're having sex with your own? Go ahead. 'Fess up. And don't feel too guilty about it because I can assure you he does it all the time.

Now, before you file for divorce, it's not such a strange thing as you might think. And it's certainly common among men and women. For men, this often takes the form of a Marilyn Monroe-like starlet from the fifties. For women, it's more likely to take the shape of a heroic movie character, like Tom Cruise or maybe a debonair, suave gentleman like George Clooney. My customer-turned-close friend Rachel, a true romantic and history buff, salivates over the thought of anything halfway handsome in armor and a sword. So go ahead, take Robin Hood to bed!

Now that we've got that out of the way and you've openly admitted you do fantasize about another man during sex, breathe. Ever thought of sharing your fantasy man fantasy with your lover? No, I didn't think so. Well, maybe it's time to give it a try. It will certainly send a little shock wave through the status quo of a humdrum bedroom existence and inject a little excitement into something that may have become mundane.

Of course, such a venture requires a great deal of trust. If there is a lack of trust or inherent jealousy in one or both of the partners, you may do more harm than good. However, if there is trust, stability, and fidelity in the relationship, sharing your fantasy man fantasy can be interesting, not to mention titillating. Believe it or not, some men do fantasize about their women with another man. They may just be more open to this than you think. There's only one way to find out.

But first, before you exclaim your fantasy with wild abandon, consider these important things:

- Ask yourself, "Am I willing to share his sexual mind with another woman?" Turnabout is fair play after all, and nobody likes a double standard, especially in the bedroom. So if you're not fully prepared to exchange tit for tat, you may not be ready for sharing your fantasy man fantasy with him. In short, if you don't think you can handle hearing his other woman fantasy, you may want to keep this door shut until you feel more confident and secure in the relationship.

- Consider whether your fantasy will make him jealous, which is not necessarily a bad thing, and to what extent. Few people know him better than you do. Is he the overly jealous type? Does he tend to get a little too possessive or even irrational when it comes to the platonic males in your life? In short, will this fantasy man endeavor create a rift of trust in him that will be hard to repair later?

- Now, with the first two considerations securely in mind, assure him before you share your fantasy that it is only that, a fantasy. Nothing more. Remind him of this as needed.

Now, who should share first? Either way, you're the icebreaker because you introduced the subject. Still, it might be preferable to approach the matter this way. Men, being what they are, tend to get complacent about their significant others. With that in mind, you might start by telling him you have a fantasy you want to share. Don't actually tell him what it is at this point. Rather, encourage him to share his other woman fantasy first. If he denies he has one, tell him you know better and you weren't born yesterday. But reassure him that you don't mind. It's only natural. Everyone has them, especially nowadays when computers are so readily available that they give men an assortment of women to fantasize about.

Of course, if all his denials are sincere and he really doesn't fantasize about anyone but you, fall on your knees immediately, and thank your Maker for such a treasure of golden manhood. But since men like this don't exist (except in our fantasies!), he'll most likely open up and react with enthusiasm at the idea of swapping such imaginings.

Now, why is it usually best to let him share his other person fantasy first?

- If you go first and he gets heatedly jealous or angry right off the bat, you've done some damage that will be a pain to repair. Moreover, he can now seize the opportunity of assuming the moral high ground on the subject of mental fidelity while secretly enjoying his own other person fantasy.
- If he shares his fantasy first, then he can say nothing about yours when it is your turn. That is, once he shares his other person fantasy, he pretty much forfeits his right to complain about yours. Think of it as disarming him beforehand and taking away his weapon.

Just don't let yourself get jealous when he starts talking about Jenifer Lopez (a.k.a. J-Lo) shaking her booty on stage! Remember, you opened this door.

Now it's your turn. Again, how and when you choose to share your fantasy is up to you. What's your personality? If it's easier for you to whisper it in safe darkness a little at a time into his ear, then do that. How about writing it down and letting him read it when you're not around? Or let him read it when you are right next to him. He may see you as another woman at this point. Are you an artist? Draw him a picture. Or cut some pictures illustrating your fantasy and leave them in his underwear drawer. Add a perfumed suggestive note or photo of yourself with your fantasy man. Or, if it's his other woman fantasy, a photo of you dressed as a fifties bombshell or whatever turns him on. Maybe this would be a good time to visit your local costume shop and bring home an outfit he won't soon forget. Don't forget the wig!

What about timing? You can swap fantasies before you have sex, enjoying the awareness of knowing you're both indulging in them while you're making love. Or you can take turns, waiting until the next time you have sex when the other person can open up. This can certainly maintain suspense, which can enhance one's pleasure when it comes. This can be a game of "You owe me next time." Whatever route you take, remember to keep your mind open at all times, keeping in your mind and his that this exercise is for fun and fun only. Just remember to have fun and "Get your groove on, girl!"

Real-Life Story

I recently had a female customer in who is recently divorced and has two boys. She has shopped with me for quite some time. This particular time, she came in with a man that she introduced as her friend. After the introduction, she started showing him the lingerie area. I went on about my business, thinking maybe this was a new boyfriend and she was hinting at some lingerie gifts. I went back to check on them to find her standing outside the dressing room in a very crystal clear negligee. I could see everything, and I do mean everything! It was almost like she was standing there naked, and she was standing in a three-way mirror so there really was not anything he could not see. I was very embarrassed, so I decided to just stay out of the way. What else could I have done? I certainly was left speechless, so I tried to fade into the background.

I found out that he was not her boyfriend. He was her son's soccer coach. And yes, you guessed it, he was married! Maybe it was his or her fantasy, but I am just suggesting that maybe you should make sure you are the one in your husband's fantasy. Make sure you give him a little lingerie fashion show.

Apart from the sexual excitement involved in this venture, this sharing of your other man fantasy can help keep your man from getting too comfortable in your affections. Most men possess a King Kong-sized ego. A man rarely considers the possibility that his wife or girlfriend may find a man besides him attractive. Most likely, he probably has been thinking all this time that he is the only one fantasizing about another person. It won't do him any harm to know you are, too. So think of this other man fantasy exercise, besides being a phenomenal spice in your sex life, as something of an equalizer, a tool in keeping those nasty double standards at bay. My great-grandmother used to say, "What's good for the goose is good for the gander!"

Oh Santa Baby! (Your Sex Wish List)

Don't you just love getting a letter? Not a cold, impersonal email. Not an impersonal note scratched out on an old notepad. Not a messy, hard-to-read message scrawled across a paper napkin. A real letter. Especially when it's on nice stationary that smells faintly perfumey. Oh, we love to savor the mystery of the contents, breathless upon opening it. Well, your man would love a letter, too, especially when the contents of the letter, once opened, pertains to sex. Well, there it is. You're about to write a letter to your lover. Actually, your letter will be a list, your sex wish list to be precise. It's like when you tell your children to make out their Christmas lists. Well, now's the time for your own. Don't leave anything you may want from him off the list either. Now is the time to really let loose. Who knows? Maybe it will be something he also wishes for.

First, dig out that gorgeous stationary you've been keeping in a shoebox in the guest room closet. Now, take a sheet of stationary paper, and compose a list of three or more things you wish your man would do to you in bed, before, during, or after sex, something like "seduce me using only your fingers" or "speak to me like a . . ." Remember, men love dirty talk.

Put some thought in it. Put some thought in it. Oops, did I say that twice? Good, I meant to. Remember, these wishes represent those romantic, sexual or not, things you've always wanted done, things you know do or will excite and please you. Perhaps you were afraid to ask for them before. Well, here is a sexy way to get around your shyness. To be sure, there is always room for individual tastes and personality. Phrase your wishes subtly or boldly or suggestively or frankly. Whatever you do, be honest. Add whatever props like a thong, picture, chocolate, or sexy photograph of you in lingerie. Now put whichever one or maybe all of them in the envelope you think will illustrate your message.

When finished, spray a little of his favorite perfume of yours over the paper. Be careful now, especially if the contents of your letter are particularly "flammable." You don't want to ignite the whole thing. Fold it and insert it in a matching envelope—yes, *matching*, young lady! You want him to know you relished the task of creating this intriguing little missive and you put some thoughtful care into making it pleasing to his senses. Now, for the pièce de résistance, go put on some red lipstick and seal your wish list envelope with a kiss. Let the lipstick imprint fall across the sealed seam. Write "Sealed with a lick and kiss."

Here's another suggestion. If you really want to be creative and foster a little sexy intrigue, consider writing your final, most daring wish in French. I mean, sexy, romantic things always sound better in French, right? This little mystery will arouse his curiosity and relentlessly tease his imagination. (Don't spoil the suspense by telling him.) He may not know what the words mean yet, but he knows it'll be something good. Once he discovers the erotic/sexy meaning of the words, he'll be more than eager to translate your little wish into pleasurable reality.

Now, from this point, you have several options. Make it a game in bed, that is, right when you're ready for sex. Or later, the next time he wants to have sex and you may not be particularly ready, pull out the envelope, and tell him to pick one of your wishes.

15

Reach for the Razor

I was watching a very funny comedy show one night on TV. And the subject came up between the husband and wife characters. She brought up that she needed to shave her legs.

He quickly replied, "I did not want to say anything to you, but they could sure use a trim!"

She said, "Are they really that bad?"

He then replied, "Well, sometimes it's like sleeping with a Christmas tree!"

Okay, let's face it. Shaving one's legs is a thorn in the feminine side. It's also something of a beauty obligation these days. We love having hairless gams but detest the effort one must put forth to get them. There are few chores so dreaded and so procrastinated. Can I go one more day without shaving?

When I was a flight attendant, that was the big joke after coming home from a four-day trip. There was lots of groaning and moaning that now legs would have to be shaved. I listened but couldn't understand because I shave my legs every day and love the way they feel. I cannot even fathom the thought of how a hairy, stubbly leg would feel.

Before you go and throw bricks at me let me explain. When I was a young girl, all my friends were shaving their legs. When I asked if I could shave mine, my mother said very loud and clear, "No!" I decided to steal one of my father's razors and hid out in my bathroom to shave them anyway. I loved how soft they felt. Of course, when my mother found out, she yelled that now I would have to shave them every single day or the hair on them would grow back darker and longer. I don't know if it was an old wives' tale or not, but you better believe me that, from that day on, I never forgot to shave my legs.

Well, here's a tip that may make you not mind so much. Shaving your legs can be a simple yet powerful turn-on for your man. The next time you shave, do it where he can watch the proceeding. Prop your leg in a sexy pose, like on the counter sink or over the rim of the tub in the bath or shower. Unhurriedly apply a sweet-smelling shaving cream. It won't hurt to let a little fall down your body, maybe landing on one of your nipples.

You could say in a sultry voice, "Oh, look what I've done. Can you wipe this off for me, dear?"

Don't forget the sexy head tilt. Back to the legs, take long, slow strokes with your razor. As you do, catch his eye, intentionally or accidentally, and respond with the sultry look. At intervals during the shaving, slowly slide your hand up and down your leg to test the smoothness. When you're done with your leg, run your hand all the way from your ankle to the top of your thigh and even inside your thigh. Using "the voice," invite him to feel for himself how silky your legs are. Ask him to tell you if you missed a spot.

The fun doesn't stop there. When you get out of the tub or shower (*if* you get out of the tub or shower . . . wink, wink), prop your legs on the sink or bed where he can watch you massage fragrant lotion onto them. Or let him do it if he appears so inclined.

Of course, this may or may not lead to sex right then. Either way, it will certainly give him something to think about during the day. The moment-to-moment knowledge that there is a pair of soft, smooth, and willing legs under your clothes, combined with the memory of your suggestiveness while shaving them, is pure magic. It will keep him expecting that good things are sure to follow within the next twenty-four hours or before the stubble grows back, whichever comes first. Now, go shave your legs!

You are now done. Was that not wickedly easy? I know from experience that the payoff of this little exercise and others like it that we've examined will far outweigh the time (five minutes, tops!).

While we are on the subject of shaving, if you are planning a romp in the boudoir and your man needs some of those stubbles taken off, you can offer to shave him. It can be a really fun way to make sure that, when he rubs his face all over your body parts, it is soft as a baby's butt. Or maybe you both can shave each other.

Men love to be surprised in the shower by the way. It catches them off guard in a delightful, exciting way. Surprise is the remedy for predictability and replaces those mundane times. You can spray his chest with shaving cream and use it to write dirty words all over his body. If your man is a hairy man (and perhaps sometimes a bit much in certain areas), this would be a good time to man-scape him.

Also, for you ladies who have a bit more than you need, don't wait until bikini season. Please keep the bushes trimmed. Like your legs, your flower should not have thorns. You never know when the moment will occur for intimacy, so why not just keep yourself manicured like a well-kept lawn, neatly hedged all the time.

Believe me, ladies. In the years I have seen women in the dressing room, I cannot tell you how many look like they have grown an entire yard. (If you are one of the women whose husband does not like to go down there, maybe you should take a look.) Also, a monthly squirt of Eve douche can keep your flower smelling as fresh as a daisy and much more inviting when he goes down to that Garden of Eden to touch and smell your flower.

I won't promise that you'll love shaving your legs from now on. There's no hope for that! Still, when you see how powerful this little turn-on exercise can be, you may not dread it so much each time you pick up your razor. The concept is simple. Take an unpleasant task, and give it an enjoyable, romantic twist. After all, sex can make any activity more interesting. Or is it the other way around?

My friend Melody, who not only shaves her legs and underarms daily, but she shaves her rose petals, as she calls it. She loves the soft as a babies butt feelings. She shared with me the secret to the fastest and safest way to shave and still get the result you want. She only uses the razors with the built-in shaving cream, which cuts her time in half because she does not have to lather up her legs with cream from a can. They also keep you lathered so there is less chance of razor burn or nicks. Where she is shaving, that is the last place you want to knick. I can tell you that I did go out and purchase the product, and now I am hooked as well.

16

On Bended Knee

A man's first love is his own penis. Some people believe the man's brain is inside his penis, and for the most part, that is true. Take President Bill Clinton, for example. He was smart enough to get elected president but let his penis rule. It's also been said that the seat of a man's soul resides in the penis. I'm not that accurate in the terminology, but it's pretty damn close. Men grew up touching their buddy from the first moment they realized it was dangling there. It was their companion in bed, under the bed, or in the bath, basically any place they could hide and get away to play with it. Men never stop touching their penis by the way. Even when they are out in public every now and then, you will catch a grown man touching himself, and even on TV, you will catch the football players scratching during a game.

Here's a secret. Okay, well, it's not a secret. It's a fact everyone knows but likes to pretend ignorance. Men masturbate until they die. Some have died while doing it, for that matter. Depending on the man, it's not always a pretty picture to envision. So we make ourselves believe that our man does not, but believe me. He does!

If a man denies it, bet your bottom dollar he's lying. Oh, yeah, he's good with his hands. But there's one thing he can't do with it.

He can't suck it! If he could, he would. Boy, do they want to. How frustrating for them. Poor little dears.

Male dogs do it all the time because they can. Haven't you ever heard a man's remark when he catches a dog licking himself? "I would do it if I could" they all say and laugh out loud.

At any rate, this nature-barred method of self-pleasuring can be a great source of release for him and a sure way to use the wisdom you have to ask for jewelry as a reward. Conventional wisdom maintains that jewelry is sometimes birthed in this way. It could definitely be the way to get him to pay off that bracelet you have on layaway. I can promise you that, when you give your man a little oral pleasure, he will give you some retail pleasure.

Enter woman. Well, you woman, not the other woman. You don't have to love it. (You do, however, have to love him.) Changing poopy diapers ain't no fun either. You do it, however, because the little tot can't. One day, he'll appreciate you for it. The perk of this deed is that your man will appreciate it now. So even if giving head is not your favorite thing, my advice is to suck it up (pun intended) and do it. The rewards might be worth the little time spent on your knees. I promise it really won't take long, especially if you have never or if you don't usually pleasure him.

But take heart, my dears, there are ways to make the experience more tasteful, figuratively and literally. Purchase an edible oil or scented lotion. This can also make it more enjoyable for you because men can sometimes smell a little sweaty down there all cooped up in their pants all day, so rubbing something scented on it can make it much more pleasurable for you. Some taste very nice indeed, like strawberries and cream or chocolate mint, for example. Put a small fingertip-sized amount on the head. Any more than that can create a mess. With the oil, massage his penis into an erection with your hand(s). Let the tip of your tongue flicker over and around the head. Slowly slide your mouth down over his shaft as far as possible, stopping short of the gagging point. Don't worry. In time, you will learn where all your barriers are, and your comfort level will rise. If you need a visual, rent the movie *Deep Throat*. You may just learn a few new techniques!

Now, if you ask one hundred men what their favorite sexual act would be, I'll bet most would say oral sex. If you enjoy giving your man head, he is one lucky guy. But if you just can't get past the gagging part of it to enjoy it yourself, try this method. Take his penis in your mouth and slide it in as deep as possible but not so far that you feel that gag response. Then slowly take it out, but keep your lips wrapped around the head of it. Now, this is the most crucial part. BREATHE! Breathe in through your nose and out through your mouth. But as you exhale, begin to slide his penis back down your throat. A little trick I heard about in one of the erotica books I read was to lie on your back with your head slightly hanging off the bed. This allows your muscles in your throat to open and relax. It also allows you to take more of his penis. He can straddle you on the bed or stand up against the bed in case he needs to balance himself or his knees get weak. This also allows you to have your hands free to fondle and squeeze his penis and balls. When giving your guy a blow job, try making some loud moaning sounds. Let him feel like there is nothing else in the world you would rather be doing at that very moment than sucking on his manhood. For those of you who really would rather be doing anything else in the world, this will help hurry the deed.

Men love to see their penis cupped between your breasts. So maybe you could give him a few thrilling minutes of letting him watch you slide his penis up and down between them. It will help get his motor started and help you finish earlier in the end.

A great way to get him excited before you start the deed and to assure that it will go more quickly is for you start with a tease. Men love the feel of lingerie, so use a piece of your lingerie to excite him. First stand in front of him and slowly pull down your panties. After you drop them down around your ankles, turn around with your buttocks facing him, and slowly bend over from the waist. Pull them off and toss them in his face. Men also get aroused from the scent of a woman, like wild animals do. Walk sultry over to him, and take your panties back from him. Push him back on the bed or whatever piece of furniture or floor is closest to you. Take your panties and wrap them around his penis, and slide your hand up and down his shaft. This will surely excite him, especially if you stop every few seconds to lean down and kiss the head of his penis.

Now, if the very thought of putting his penis in your mouth or down your throat still makes you gag, just try not to even think about it. You can always do the next best thing. Play with it. Tease it using your lips and tongue as well as your hands and fingers. (Men love to watch their penis grow, so engage him and make sure you allow him the opportunity of watching with a good view if possible.) Take it in your hands, and stroke your face with it. Then kiss and lick some more. Remember, the head is very sensitive, so go easy there, and keep the contact light. You can take his testicles in your hand and gently squeeze them, or if they are easy accessible, you can also lick around them, too. Men love to see a woman's face while they are being given head, so make sure you look into his eyes some and linger a little, giving him the sexy, sultry look.

If you are one of the many women who really prefer not to give your man a blow job, then I will share a great secret with you. Joie, a customer who used to be an escort, revealed to me that she made most of her money by giving head. Although she did not really mind it so much, she did not ever want to swallow. She would just let the cum slowly spill down her arm and wipe it against her body to wash off later, or she would let it fill her mouth. But as she slowly pulled his penis out of her mouth, she would cup her one hand and let the cum fall into her hand. She would discreetly dispose of it as she excused herself to go into the bathroom.

She told me that under no circumstances should you ever tell your man you hate performing oral sex on him or you don't want to swallow. You will just hurt his feelings because the man's sperm is, in his mind, as precious as his penis. Her favorite way (and the easiest) was to climb into the shower and coax your man in with you. Strategically place him with the shower pulsating on his back with you, kneeling on the shower floor while facing him. Maneuver yourselves where the water flowing will be just enough to act like a gentle waterfall down his chest and onto his genital area. (You'll understand and appreciate the waterfall in a minute.) You can then make this fun and ensure he is squeaky clean at the same time. Grab some scented soap, and start washing his penis and his balls. Let your fingers slowly slide between his butt cheeks. Gently play and stroke his man parts.

His engine will soon jump-start, which will make your ride a shorter one, if you know what I mean. When you feel he is getting close to the finish line, start licking around the head and gently suck on his balls, one at a time. Then when you know he is for sure ready to explode, suck on his penis as you slide it in and out of your mouth. When you can, let a trickle of water get in your mouth from the waterfall stream. This will make his penis more slippery, which is more like the feel of your vagina. Plus, it will give a fresh rinse of your mouth while you're waiting for him to ejaculate. Once he does and you don't wish to swallow, just let the liquid slowly mix with the water in your mouth and drip out and down the drain with all the suds. No one will be the wiser!

17

Yes, I Said "Masturbation"

Does the word "masturbation" get your attention? Did you know that men love to watch a woman masturbate? Besides the threesome or a "ménage a trois," which is at the top of most men's sexual wish list, watching a woman masturbate is definitely next in lineage. Some women feel silly or embarrassed about masturbation and feel it is something that should be done alone, behind closed doors, or in the dark. But if you can make yourself get past those feelings, masturbation can be an enlightening and liberating feeling, not to mention a great way to show your partner how you like to be touched.

Turn the lights down low or light a candle, preferably a well-scented one. Sit back against a cozy, plush pillow or, even better, on the couch or comfy chair. Just to be out of the norm, start touching and cupping your breasts and gently pull on your nipples. If you can muster up the courage, talk softly and again, with a Marilyn Monroe voice. Teach him while you tell him what you are doing and how it feels. Spread your legs and bend your knees up until the heels of your feet are touching your buttocks. Pull gently on your clitoris, and flick it with your fingernail. Then tell him to watch as you very slowly slide one and then two fingers into your vagina. This will be sure to drive you both wild. If you are not yet ready to have sex, remember you are finally in control. Just flip yourself over on all fours, take one hand, reach back, and smack your ass. I don't know of any man who would stop a show like that, so just keep it up, that is, until you are ready for it. This is also a great time to introduce him to a vibrator if you haven't already.

For those of you who have never ever masturbated or maybe feel it is a sin, let me reassure you that it is not! Not only is masturbation healthy, especially for ladies who do not have a partner, it can be a learning experience. If you know what turns you on, then you can better tell or guide your man to things you like and that work for your body. Here are a few tips:

1. Take a tub ride. If you have jets in your tub, then you are a very lucky lady. Hot tubs are also fun. Just move your body to where the jets are, and move to the position that most stimulates your private areas. If you are not lucky enough to have either, don't panic. Just lie back in your tub, and turn the water to a temp that will not be too hot. Let the stream of warm water take you away. If you are not getting the stimulation that you need, gently pull back your vaginal lips so the water can touch more of your clitoris. If you are in a hot tub, you can get closer to the jet if you like a more intense stimulation or, of course, move a little further away if you like it less intense.

2. Give yourself a slow erotic massage. Next time you know you will be alone for a while and no one will be knocking on your door, grab some massage oil, and lie back on something soft and comfy. Light some candles. This will give you more of a calm environment. Start by rubbing some oil on your arms and legs. Make sure to rub softly and slowly. Take the time. Your body will thank you later. Rub the rest of your body, and don't forget your buttocks. But make sure that you leave your genitals for last because the more you work yourself up, the more intense your orgasm will be. If you

can position yourself in front of a mirror, this will add to the erotic mood you will soon be experiencing.

3. Use props. Grab a soft pillow and some soft fabric like silk or satin. Get on your knees, put the pillow between your legs, and start rubbing your clitoris back and forth over it. Then take the fabric, and twist it into a rope. Hold one end with one hand and the other with your other hand. Again on your knees, take the fabric, and run it all the way to one end until the fabric can't go any further. Then take it back to starting position very slowly. After you get some excitement going, you can go a little faster until you reach orgasm.

4. Explore your body. Purchase some warming oil or lotion for this tip because warm sensations heighten the orgasm. Lie back and spread your legs as far as you can. You can either lay them on the bed or take them high in the air. Start by applying some of the warming oil on the outer vaginal lips and start caressing this area. (It is very sensitive, and men sometimes forget it.) After you softly touch in that area, start with the inner area of your vaginal lips. Rub and stroke your clitoris with the fingers of your other hand, and don't forget to put a finger or two inside your vagina. I recently sold some anal lubrication to a lady, and she said she never lets her lube run out because, when she masturbates, she likes to insert a finger in her rectum because the orgasm she gets is a much more explosive one.

5. Lie on your back, and let your head hang over the side of the bed. The blood flowing to your head will intensify your orgasm. Take a few pillows, and slide them under your butt to tilt your pelvis upward. Keeping your legs together, slide your finger in and out of your vagina and up and down on your clitoris and also in a circular motion. When you are about to have an orgasm, replace your fingers with your vibe, and rub it up and down slowly, adding more friction. As your excitement heightens, the vibrator will make your orgasm a much more intense one.

6. Find your G-spot, ladies, that is, if there really is one. Some women have shared with me their experience of finding their magnificent spot and how exciting and more profound their orgasm was. If you are one of those lucky ladies who do experience a G-spot orgasm, good for you! If you have not yet experienced this so-called explosive orgasm or if you cannot find your G-spot, try inserting a finger and curling it like you are calling someone over with your finger. If you still cannot find it, may I recommend purchasing a G-spot vibe. This vibe is only a few inches long, and it has a slight arch. Insert it with the curved side pointing upward toward your belly, and move it gently around in a circle or in and out like a penis. I recommend a jelly G-spot vibe because they are soft and more realistic.

7. If you are against a vibrator, just use your fingers. Try reading a book on erotica, and when you start to get excited, start touching yourself and keep reading. You will find yourself emerged in the fantasy and easier to have an orgasm. It can take you to "La La Land" and where work and bills just don't exist.

If you dare, let your man watch any and all of the above. Men love to watch their ladies touch themselves.

Every Girl Needs a Vibe

A wise fashionista once quipped that no woman should be without a little black dress in her wardrobe. I say no woman should be without a vibrator in her wardrobe. Just think of it as your "little black dress" of sex. Make no mistake. This is an essential accessory in your intimacy ensemble.

Not only may it be discreetly tucked away in the same closet with your clothes or hidden in the bottom of your laundry basket (safe from children or nosy friends and family), this wonder of modern invention can caress your most sensitive places, and some vibes are as soft as silk. It will take you into any season (single, between boyfriends, and so forth) and is appropriate for any occasion within your romantic social calendar. Make an even bolder statement by pairing it with an exotic scented oil (preferably the warming kind) or massage lotion. It's surprisingly easy to care for, too. It is not, however, machine washable.

Like lamp shades, these handy and sadly underrated devices come in a variety of shapes, sizes, textures and colors. And trust me, you need one. So just what specifically is so useful about these little gadgets?

First of all, at the risk of stating the obvious, they are a companion (of sorts) when a girl finds herself alone, languishing in a thirsty desert of unfulfilled desire. That is, if you can't enjoy a vibrating hand, you can at least enjoy a handy vibrator. Just a note about the history of the vibrator. They were first invented back in the Victorian era by a doctor who used them to treat women who suffered from hysteria. So ladies, even way back then, a good climax was critical for the health of a woman.

Real-Life Story

I'll share an actual story that happened one day in my shop a few years ago. I was in the middle of stocking what I call my "Exotic Room," discreetly tucked away. While in the middle of putting some vibrators in the drawers, a lady came into the store and was just looking around. I asked her if I could help her, and she said no. She was just looking and had just discovered my shop. I let her browse for a while, and when she came into the area I was in, she could not help but notice the items I was stocking.

She said very quietly, "I have never seen things like this before!"

One conversation led to another and to the merchandise I was holding in my hand. I explained to her that I sell items like this all day long and have to constantly place new orders. She just was totally amazed. She said very meekly that she had never masturbated before in her life. She had married at a very early age, and her husband had been the only one she had ever even slept with. They were married for thirty-seven years. Unfortunately, he had passed away two years ago.

Before I knew it, my mouth just took over. Of course, I did not stop to think about what I was saying. I just blurted out, "Boy, you must be a pretty stressed-out woman!" I can't even imagine having no sexual release for over two years.

That is when I introduced her to the Wascally Wabbit. "If you purchase this and put in three C batteries, you will think you have died and gone to heaven!"

She, of course, was reluctant. She replied "Oh, I don't know, I am a very religious person and I'm not sure it would be the right thing to do."

I told her, as I took hold of her hand. "If God did not want you to enjoy your clitoris, he would not have given it to you."

After a little more convincing, I talked her into the little gadget. I felt very proud and liberated for her and could hardly wait for her to get the thrill of her life.

About two weeks later, she appeared in front of me and whispered, "Remember me?"

I said, "Yes, I do remember you. How have you been?"

She then said quietly, "I am the one you made buy the vibrator."

I was a little nervous at this point. Maybe she hated it. Maybe it did not own up to my personal guarantees. But to my surprise, not only did she thank me, she told me she loved it. Not only did she love it, she had spent the entire weekend in bed. (That Wascally Wabbit!)

So ladies, there is nothing wrong with owning a good vibe. It can be the foot massage you wished your man would give you. It can rub your tired neck at night, and it can be a fun way to spend time with yourself in the shower. More importantly, it will not let you down. You will have an orgasm and a good one.

Note to customers: There are no returns or exchanges on any toys. It is an FDA warning/regulation.

By the way, toys are not just for women. I was told men enjoy them as well.

Real-Life Story

One of my friends, Scarlett, had caught her husband cheating. Well . . . not red-handed but let's say the lacy black thongs she found peeking out from under their bed was NOT hers! After being divorced over six years, and not having been in an intimate relationship, she was feeling particularly lonely one night. She pulled out her trusty (and dusty) old vibe, only to discover it had dead batteries. Along with her marriage, it too was dead. Desperate, she turned instead to another item, the vibrating handle of her electric toothbrush! I say, "Whatever works for you." The lesson learned here is to always keep an extra supply of batteries.

Next, if you're one of those women who climax easily vaginally, then this next paragraph may not apply to you. The rest of us here on Planet Earth hate you by the way. Most Earth girls, you see, rely on the clitoral variety of orgasm. Even then, to further frustrate us, most of us sadly have a difficult time getting the necessary clitoral stimulation we need to climax during intercourse, especially when we're arranged in body positions reminiscent of pretzels and Celtic knots.

Enter the handy vibe. It certainly would have worked have for Scarlett, had she remembered to have extra batteries on hand. Holding this little rescuer to the clitoris will certainly bring you an orgasm to remember. Watch for falling rocks! For you *Sex and the City* devotees, you'll remember Samantha's favorite model, "the Rabbit." It looks like a soft jelly penis with a realistic head with rabbit ears midway down that wiggle and dance to massage your clitoris and other areas. It will certainly make you hop! Pleasure pearls in the see-through shaft spin and rotate.

Samantha talked about how she worshiped that little thing on many an episode. On one episode, she enjoyed her rabbit so much that she refused to leave her bedroom. I always tell my customers who ask which vibe is my personal favorite. I am very happily married, but I do love my "Wascally Wabbit." There are, however, so many now to choose from. Vibes are like accessories. You can never have too many.

Real-Life Story

Shelly, a flight attendant friend of mine, stopped by my boutique on her way home from a trip. She told me she had to purchase another Wascally Wabbit.

I asked, "Didn't you just purchase one a few weeks ago?"

She laughed and said, "Yes, but you will not believe what happened to me on my four-day trip."

I couldn't wait to hear the story since she was talking so fast with excitement in her voice. I was all ears. She told me that she had decided that, since she would be on a long trip that had lots of long nights, she would pack her wabbit. On one of the layovers, she and the other flight attendants, along with the two pilots, were walking through the airport when her suitcase hit one of the speed bumps. All of a sudden, her suitcase started humming.

One of the pilots asked, "Shelly, is that your suitcase I hear?"

Of course, she knew the vibe must have turned itself on when it hit the bump. She ran as fast as she could to the nearest ladies' room and said she could not get her suitcase open fast enough. When she got to the humming toy, she was so embarrassed because, of course, other women were in there. The only thing she could think of was to get rid of it. She said she just threw it into the nearest trash can, closed her suitcase, ran out of there, and got onto the plane as fast as she could.

I said to her, "I would have just died."

Shelly laughed and said she almost did. She hung out for most of the trip in the back of the airplane. So ladies, if you do ever take your vibrator on a trip with you, please remove the batteries.

I have a few more suggestions of toys that will rock your world:

- **G-Spot Tickler:** Japan's number-one thumb-controlled multispeed vibe for maximum enjoyment. It's small in size, but it sends your clitoris and G-spot to ecstasy.
- **The Jungle Juggler:** A high-power jelly, soft, flexible, textured vibe. It is a wild, gyrating ride.
- **Tickler:** A device shaped like the penis with a little butterfly that stimulates the clitoris.
- **WE Vibe:** The world's most popular vibrator for couples. It is designed to be worn while making love.
- **The Pocket Rocket:** A device that fits in your purse for easy travel. It is no larger than a tampon but much more delightful.
- **The Magic Bullet:** A silver egg-shaped bullet on a cord that extends to a remote control that allows you to control the speed of the vibration while you move about tending to your daily chores.
- **The Venus Butterfly:** A device that is easily worn during lovemaking. It is reversible with adjustable straps. Your clitoris will flutter into ecstasy on your erogenous zone.
- **Ben Wa Balls:** A tool that was invented hundreds of years ago to enhance sexual stimulation when inserted into the vagina during sexual intercourse. They also have the benefit of strengthening the Kegel muscles. Try this out for fun the next time you are cleaning house. Insert them, and grab the vacuum cleaner. If you can learn to keep them in while vacuuming, that will be an extra chore done. Just don't forget to take them out if Aunt B calls to pick her up in the airport gate. I don't think they will get past security!

These are just a few. There are so many to choose from that it will blow your mind. It might be your newest shopping addiction. So come on, girls. Spice things up. Give the gift of pleasure to you and your man.

Last but not least, it may also surprise you to find that this little device can also bring untold pleasure to your man. Don't believe me? Give it a try before you abandon the idea. Next time you're in the bedroom with your lover, just run your vibe gently along his penis down to the scrotum area and in between his legs, not necessarily in that sequence. (Warning: Tread lightly on the head. It's very sensitive.)

Two recent studies from Indiana University say that, not only is the use of vibrators during sexual activity a common practice, it could also have some health benefits. The male and female studies conducted among adult Americans show 45 percent of men saying they've used a vibrator, with most of the heterosexual men surveyed saying they had done so during foreplay or intercourse with a female partner. Roughly 17 percent of the male respondents said they had used a vibrator for solo masturbation. The studies show that 53 percent of women frequently use vibrators.

According to the *Medical News (www.News-Medical.net)* "Vibrator use during sex is common, linked to sexual health" *published June 30, 2009)*, the studies, "led by researchers at the Center for Sexual health promotion in IU's School of Health, Physical Education and Recreation," are the first to publish data about vibrator use from nationally representative samples of the American population. This lack of data has existed despite a longstanding practice by many physicians and therapists to recommend vibrator use to help treat sexual dysfunctions or to improve sexual enjoyment.

In addition to demonstrating the common use of vibrators, the studies also found that respondents associated the use of vibrators with more positive sexual function and saw the devices as tools for being more proactive about their sexual health.

"The Study about women's vibrator use affirms what many doctors and therapists have known for decades that vibrator use is common, it's linked to positive sexual function such as desire and ease of orgasm, and it's rarely associated with any side effects," Debby Herbenick, associate director of the Center for Sexual Health Promotion, told news reporters.

Michael Reece, director of the Center for Sexual health promotion, told *Medical News* that the studies are important for the contributions they make to an understanding of the sexual behaviors and sexual health of adults in today's society. "The study about male vibrator use is additionally important because it shows that vibrator use is also common among men, something that has not been documented before," Reece said.

The studies, which involved 2,056 women and 1,047 men aged eighteen to sixty, were funded by Church & Dwight Co. Inc., maker of Trojan brand sexual health products.

So while the law says you may not return a vibrator after purchase, it is not, however, against the law to own one. So ladies, don't waste any more time finding the perfect one for you. Remember, orgasms are a natural gift, so like the ex-flight attendant in me, I will say, "Before takeoff, sit back, relax, and enjoy the flight!" For you ladies who are still a little skeptical, please reread the above study.

18

Sex Over Sixty or Seventy or Eighty (and Beyond)

Sex after sixty (and beyond)? Yes, Virginia, it does exist. And yes, you can still have it. And you should have it. It really does burn calories. It is common knowledge that any exercise that will raise your heart rate for at least twenty minutes a day several times a week is helpful. If you just hate the thought of exercising, then without destroying your home, may I suggest that you can chase your spouse around the table! You'll be surprised how much younger you will look and feel. It will also give you a lot more confidence, and it is essential as we grow older that we also keep in shape.

My mother-in-law, now ninety-one, is a fine testament to that. She has been working out and walking all her life. She still does, and she still drives. If you don't use it, you will lose it. Think about it.

It is very important for us ladies to not only work out but to keep ourselves in shape and limber. But we also need to remember to drink eight-plus glasses of water a day to help keep our skin stay moist and our fine lines plump. And don't forget to use three—to five-pound weights and work your muscles at least four days a week. If you don't, your body will get mushy, and then there goes your self-confidence, not to mention your health. Women who work out weekly and stay in shape are more likely to not only look better as they age but stay more sexually involved. Men are just plain lucky that they don't have the cellulite and dimples we ladies get, but using weights will keep you more toned. I so believe that, when we look better, our sex drive is better. I think it helps us mentally when we work out because, not only does it make us healthier, it also releases endorphins to our brain, and that definitely stimulates us.

We women aren't the only humans who lose confidence and grow self-conscious as we age. Perhaps your man has lost his hair, wears bifocals, or has gone up a pant size or two. He worries he may not be the pillar of virile manhood he once was or thought he was, especially now if the overwhelming emotional and physical passion of your earlier days or years has mellowed to a comfortable complacency or even (shame on you) physical negligence on your part. He may doubt his power to turn you on as he once did. He may doubt he is still desirable to you as a man. And that, my friend, is dangerous. The other woman may even now be lurking in the shadows. (And yes, I am trying to scare you.) Plenty of single, lonely, and desperate women out are there longing to do the things to and with your man that you are refusing to do. Don't let them borrow your husband.

I was recently attending a wedding at the beach in Hilton Head. A lady whom I did not know approached me, and we started talking about how beautiful the wedding was. I could not help but notice how striking she was. Her shoulder-length, all-grey hair was blowing in the wind, as was her flowing, long skirt. I remember also how beautiful her blue eyes were and how meticulous her makeup was. During our conversation, I found out that this stunning woman was seventy-nine. I was so surprised because she certainly did not seem that old at all. The word "matronly" was definitely not used to describe her.

That day, I decided I would not let age get the best of me. So remember, ladies, no matter how old you are, presentation matters. This woman reminded me of a classic, older, red convertible, ageless and fun as hell.

Don't be fooled thinking that a midlife crisis can't happen to you. Trust me. When you least expect it, it will jump up and bite you right in your ass. Thank God that I managed to live through mine with no vanity car purchased. Men certainly go through it, too, hence the older man and the younger woman. I know you've seen that scenario before. I believe it's where the terms "sugar daddy" and "gold digger" come from. The guy is usually running to the car dealership at the first sign of grey hair or balding to pick out that shiny, new, red convertible. I've seen plenty of bald, older guys myself lately in different makes of convertibles, out cruising for some eye candy.

Graceful aging takes work. You have to breathe. Find your center. Take yoga classes. The stretches will help keep you limber, and your man will love that.

Here are a few tips to make you look graceful and feminine. If you are like most of us over sixty who hate our arms and don't want to expose them, there are tops and dresses that have the sleeves with cutouts down the entire sleeve or around the shoulder, which not only hide the unsightly but are really very sexy in a classy way. Some of my favorites are the sheer covers made by Petit Pois (made in the United States). They are feminine and sexy.

If you hate your legs and saggy knees, try wearing long, curvaceous skirts or long, full, flowing ones. There are long, cotton yoga skirts available. Paired with a cute cotton top, they can make a very feminine ensemble. Not only do they hide the scary, they accentuate the figure.

Also ladies, we all know as we mature, so do our feet. Therefore, we should give them some TLC. Most men love feet, especially bare feet with pretty, polished toes. Some men even love to suck on a woman's toes. Here is some friendly advice. Take the time, especially in the summer, to get your toenails polished. It really makes your feet sexy. I see many women who rarely paint their toenails. Since I first started wearing nail polish, I cannot ever remember not having my toenails match my nail polish. I have never done this for a man.

It just makes me feel more feminine. It really only takes less than five minutes, but with that said, at our age ladies . . . we DESERVE being treated to a pedicure. Not only will you feel like a new woman, but what a difference it makes when you accidentally wear open toe shoes. And I know how it embarrasses other women because, when ladies shop my boutique for shoes, I have often heard them say, "I guess I should get my toenails polished!" Some women even walk around with remnants of badly worn polish on their toes. Ugh!

And ladies, never forget perfume. It intoxicates the male senses. Add a dab when you get home from work or at night before you crawl into bed. That being said, there's no shame in modifying how you go about enjoying sex after sixty.

Tips for Enjoying Sex after Sixty

You

- **Find help in a bottle.** There is a new gel on the market for us women who have either reached menopause or have a little harder time getting our excitement going. It's called "Liquid V." It works like Viagra for men. It is the strongest topical female gel on the market. It is formulated to help increase blood flow to the clitoris and amplify the strength of female climax while producing a warm, tingling sensation that women love. I cannot keep it on the shelf. After just one drop of this magical gel, you will climax like hail hitting your windshield in a thunderstorm. This one, I can honestly testify that it is just awesome. It has also been FDA approved.
- **Stay off the top when making love.** No matter how good we take care of ourselves, with the relentless advance of age, gravity remains the enemy unless you've had a face lift. Not that I need to convince you of that, but it might be a wake-up call to get a realistic visual on ourselves anyway. Just to show you what I mean, take a hand mirror, and lay it on your bathroom counter. Have the smelling salts handy, be

strong, then look down into . . . WAIT . . . come back here girl! Now, breathe deeply. Don't worry. The plastic surgeon will still be here tomorrow . . . I promise! I hate to be the bearer of bad news, but when you look into that mirror, you will see what I am talking about. Gravity! It's a bitch! At least now you have some idea what he will see, so take it from me. If you climb on top, just stay upright with head straight ahead. You can, of course, look down at your man. Just watch how far you go. That's why the mirror check is important.

- **Don't forget to wear lingerie.** For a romantic evening wear a long silk or satin gown and add several long strands of pearls. For a little kinky fun, you could wear leather and lace on date night. He will love discovering it under your clothing. Love your body with lingerie, drooping boobs and all!

- **Never ever mention that his penis is not as hard anymore like it used to be.** This is a surefire way to deflate him even more. Remember, men are like little boys when their toys don't work like they wish they would. That statement will most certainly make his toy not run.

- **Remember that intercourse is not the only way to have sex.** Sometimes, just kissing, cuddling, and touching can be as satisfying as intercourse with an orgasm. Sometimes, even without an orgasm, the foreplay can be just as rewarding for many reasons. This is especially for anyone whose husband is sick or disabled. But the most important thing to remember is to keep in touch with your partner. It makes him feel like he is still the sexiest man in the world to you. Remember, he has also performance fears or may be self-conscious about his body. Well, some men are! Men just don't verbalize it like we women do. As for him, he'll deliver if you'll just be patient and a little creative as needed. Don't rush him. Enjoy him.

- **Breathe.** Find your center, take yoga classes, and remember you really need to have a workout regimen. Maybe work out together. It could be fun when you bend over to touch your toes!

"What about him?" you ask.

He's getting older, too, and things have changed in bed because of it. Remember, men over sixty have lost the youthful stud in them. But don't let him know you've figured this out. In his mind, to you, he's still the stud he always was. (You don't see him worried about walking around naked in front of you.) Let's keep it that way. There's no sense in hurting his male ego. Confidence is a critical tool for men to both enjoy sex and bring pleasure to themselves and their partners.

So what are some ways you can overcome this normal, inevitable physical change in your man and jump-start him back into youthful studliness? You can mention to him that maybe he could call his doctor and get a prescription for Viagra, you can mentally stimulate him, or you could do both. Unfortunately, men who have entered midlife may need a bit more than just to see his partner naked in order to become aroused. So you women who feel it must be your mature body that is preventing his getting turned on, stop worrying. Men can get turned on just thinking about sex, you just have to give him something to think about (and, well, maybe a little Viagra).

Him

- **Relax.** That goes for both of you. Don't focus on performance, which can only engender mood-killing stress. In fact, don't focus at all. Just let your mind and body surrender to the physical sensations going on.
- **Enjoy more foreplay time.** Did you know that rhinos take thirty days to enjoy foreplay? It's true, so we humans should at least enjoy thirty minutes. Yes, it's very sad, but many men over sixty are just now catching up to the concept of

lovemaking. Men, when they were younger, were sometimes called "slut puppies" or "whore dogs" because they wanted to always see how many women they could get into bed, just like cowboys carving another notch in their belts. Now, they too need all that extra kissing and generous caressing that we women still crave. Okay, here's a good place to reflect. Remember that certain oft-repeated lament during your salad days, namely that you don't get enough foreplay out of him. Well, now you're more likely to get it. Now that's a perk, right?

The most common issue for men over sixty sexually is, of course, erections that aren't as hard (or able to stay hard) as they once were. First of all, relax. Don't think that, because he doesn't get hard right away or he has difficulty staying erect, it's because of you or anything failing on your part. And for God's sake, don't mention he's as limp as a wet noodle. Specifically, caress his penis teasingly. Just stroke his penis and tell him how you can't wait to climb on top of it. Trust me. This is one stroke you won't mind handling. Oh, this would be the time for a little oral sex or at least a lick or two.

Real-Life Story

A retired dentist's wife shops with me every few months to only purchase lingerie. I believe they both have recently turned eighty-one. I do believe she has had a few cosmetic procedures because she certainly looks like a *young* eighty-one. She wears her hair a long shoulder-length and looks exquisite.

Sometimes, he pulls up a chair and waits while she tries on lingerie. Sometimes, he sits in the dressing room while she tries on lingerie, and sometimes, I catch him sticking his head in the curtains to catch a peek at her trying on lingerie. Last time they were in after their fun shopping escapade, she handed me a pair of lacy crotchless panties, and he picked out a pair of lace top thigh highs for her. As they approached the counter, the gleam in his eyes and the smirk on his face as he gladly handed me his money said it all. As they left holding hands, he looked back at me and said that this was one of many reasons he had married her.

I believe that is why they are still married after sixty-five years. Color me surprised! Even at eighty-one, lingerie still excites the man, and she loves to wear it for him. Imagine that my nickname for her is "Miss Fancy Pants." No matter the age, men love to see their ladies in lingerie. I guess that's where the term "dirty old man" came from.

Real-Life Story

A very prominent doctor and his wife shop with me. They too have been married forever. She buys pretty but sheer lingerie from me. While I was once helping her, she told me they were on their way to France where they owned a Chalet. I told her how lucky they were, as I had been to France several times when I was a flight attendant and loved the romantic scenery there.

We started sharing a few stories, and before I knew it, we shared what I think is their secret to such a long and happy marriage. Not only do they own a romantic chalet in France, which in itself is a tribute to their romance, they try to make time in their busy schedules to go there as often as they can to keep the spark alive. They shared with me that they sit outside on their balcony, sipping wine together. They enjoy looking at the grapevines that wind around their balcony, and they sit for hours watching the sunsets while they share stories together. And much to my surprise, they shared with me that they enjoy sitting out there naked. They also told me they take a picnic and bottle of wine to the beach every day and lie around on a towel naked.

I can only imagine that wine paired with all the nakedness and beautiful scenery can definitely keep a spark in a long relationship afire. So even if you do not own a chalet in the south of France, you can still find a vacation spot, let it all hang out, and enjoy each other's freedom. They say that fresh air is good for you, and in addition, it would be something to laugh and talk about for years to come.

Real-Life Story

A customer and her husband have been shopping with me for years. He loves to see her in sexy tops (or sexy anything for that matter) when they go out on their date nights. Over the shopping years, we have gotten to be friends and are able to joke around. On some of their shopping trips, he winks at me and whispers, "Talk Lulu into trying on this!" ("This" is a corset or sometimes a sexy bustier.) His wife is a little on the conservative side with just the right amount of shyness. She just smiles, shakes her head, and continues shopping.

On some occasions when she comes shopping alone, I will chime in, "Come on, Lulu. This would really look good on you with a pair of jeans, and you would really make your man roar like a lion."

Lulu would always tell me she wouldn't wear anything that was not bra friendly, so keeping that in mind, I made an order for some bustiers. I saw one that I knew might be just perfect for them, bra friendly for her and sexy for him. I called her up, and she came in and tried it on. I could tell by the smile on her face that this was the one. I told her that it really looked very sexy on her in a very classy way. To my surprise, she said she liked it. She said she knew he would like to see her in something like this, so with a little encouragement of course, she took it home. The next time I saw him, he was smiling that big, sheepish grin and thanking me. Then he added that he was working on her to put some streaks in her hair. While I don't really think his wife needed a lot of streaks, I felt just a few would add some sparkle to her and make her husband happy, so why not?

Her husband told me when they first met she was in her middle thirties and "Boy was she hot!" he said with a big grin covering most of his face.

"Hell, she was hot in her forties!" he bragged. He told me he still has photos of her wearing sexy things, and he pulls them out now and again to reminisce. He said "I loved seeing her in those sexy clothes and with those long and beautiful sexy legs. I love the sexy way she smiled." He even referred to her as a "tall, cool drink of water." I knew that was what he still wanted to see when he looked at her. He also told me they love to sit out on their patio and have a few martinis to relax and get his wife loosened up. On the occasions she really dresses sexy, he just loves the attention that the other men give her. It makes the "lion" in him roar. Sexy clothing can be a good way to tease your man. Just ask Lulu (or Lenny the Lion)!

Her husband, like a lot of men, would love to have more fun and spice things up a bit in the boudoir. They have been married over twenty years. She, like most women who are in their sixties, is feeling past the age of being the playmate her husband wants.

At one of our gatherings and after a few cocktails, Lulu's husband told her, "You can be as prim and proper in public all you want, but it would make my day if you would sometimes have an alter ego!"

He gives her little hints now and then what he would like. She has short blonde hair, and he would love for her to wear a long, red wig and knock on the front door. When he opens it, he wants her to say that she read in the newspaper that there was a job opening for a maid and she wanted to show him her skills. He also said he has a fantasy that she would dress as a schoolgirl and he would be the teacher. He would try to help her improve her awful grades if she would come in after school.

I personally believe when your man keeps asking for you to wear something sexy that you should (within reason). Obviously, he is voicing his desires. Wouldn't you want to be the one fulfilling them? It might just keep him out of the bagel shop, sitting in a chair and watching women go by. Remember, it's all about communication and listening, so hear him.

When I first got to really interact with his wife, it was at a girls' makeover party I hosted at the shop. After I saw how Kimberly, the makeup artist made Lulu's beautiful eyes pop with more makeup than she was used to wearing, I used this opportunity to take her from the makeup chair straight to the hair expert. His advice was much like what Lulu's husband had said. Lulu agreed to keep an open mind and think about it. She is very pale with beautiful blue eyes, but she wore her hair too light. I introduced her to my hair dresser, Heather, and hinted again.

Heather agreed that she could make her more alluring with just a tad bit of her magic colors. Lo and behold, Lulu made an appointment one day. Heather called me with excitement when Lulu also agreed that she needed a touch of color. All I can say is wow! Not only does she look younger, she's more up-to-date and definitely does not look like she is in her mid sixties.

Ladies, don't be afraid of a little change. Add some streaks to your hair if you don't want to change the entire color. What's the harm? It will grow back! By the way, her husband called and said he wanted to chase her around the sofa. He thanked me for giving his wife some extra umph and attitude. He now calls her "Lusty Locks."

The best advice I could give to any woman is, "Please play with your man!" What is the harm? I personally think it is sometimes great to pretend to be someone else, to escape from everyday humdrum activities. It's such a small request. And who knows? You might have the time of your life, and for certain, he will be having his. You have to not take life so seriously, and you have to remember that men love the tease and adventure, so make sure you are the one giving it to him. At least I say that, if he asks for something to make the relationship exciting, do your part. Some men may decide to cheat instead when they become bored.

Real-Life Story

For you ladies who have read this book so far and still don't want to believe that wearing lingerie and feminine fashions is not important at this age or stage of our life, I will share with you another story about Mr. and Mrs. Smith, who have shopped with me for the past seven years. Every Christmas Eve, right before closing, Mr. Smith walks in, wearing a cashmere trench coat and sporting a beautiful, white, sparkling smile. His silver-grey hair is combed to perfection, not a hair out of place. Even his shoes are shined and look like Italian leather. I greet him and always escort him to the lingerie department. Mr. Smith is very soft-spoken in a true Southern gentleman kind of way. We make small talk, but both know he is here to shop for his mistress and his wife for Christmas. I show him the new arrivals of my most exquisite, designer label lingerie. I pick several of my best selections and leave him for a while. He takes his time. He feels the fabric for softness, even making sure the lace isn't too scratchy. After he chooses a few nighties, he hands them to me and asks if they have matching robes. He continues shopping while I start to wrap. Mr. Smith always reminds me to put the letter M on the back side of these boxes so he doesn't mix them up with the ones for his wife. While I wrap, Mr. Smith brings up bath salts, dusting powder, warming massage oil, and a scented candle to the counter. He tells me not to worry about wrapping these and to just put them in a bag. (I assume it's for the romantic Christmas Eve rendezvous he is about to enjoy with his mistress, Ms. M.) As I go about my wrapping, Mr. Smith continues his shopping on my clearance rack for his wife. He takes less than ten minutes, brings me a ballet-length cotton gown, and asks if I would please wrap it in a different paper. I show him a couple to choose from, but he just tells me to pick. I can't help but let my mind wonder as I wrap. He sits in a chair next to my register.

I finally have to ask, "So how long have you and Mrs. Smith been married?"

I have always assumed he was married because he makes no effort to hide the gold wedding band on his left ring finger.

He quickly responds, "Almost thirty-five years."

I reply, "Wow! That's awesome!"

Mr. Smith says in a low voice, almost whisper, "Yes, she was my high school sweetheart."

I finished the wrapping and lettering of the gifts and give him the total due for all.

He then asked, "Would you mind putting the charges on a separate card?"

"Sure." I replied.

Mr. Smith asked, "What is the total for the cotton gown?"

I told him, "The total comes to $95.45, including tax."

He gave me a Visa, and then without asking the total of all the other gifts, he handed me a Gold American Express. (Men who travel usually give me this type of card.) Ms. M's gifts totaled almost five hundred dollars. I felt so sad for Mrs. Smith that I made sure her gift was wrapped with perfection. I added extra bows and a lot of trimmings. I could not help but wish she could be the other woman in her man's life. Over the past thirty-five years, had Mrs. Smith let her marriage get complacent? Had she allowed herself to take the backseat in their relationship? Although I will never know the answer to my questions, I do know that Mr. Smith is out the door of my boutique and on his way with a bag full of beautiful gifts and boudoir items perfect for a romantic Christmas Eve.

19

Final Thoughts: What Not to Share with Your Man and What to Remember to Avoid

There are so many wonderful things we can and should share with our man, but ladies, there are also many things some women share that they really should not. I have found the best rule to follow is this one. If you were on a date with a man, would you engage in conversation on any of the following?

- Don't say how bad your menstrual cramps are or how bad you're bleeding. Gross! You can let your man know that you are not feeling well without providing all the gory details. The texting expression "TMI" would apply here.
- After eating onions or some other food that leaves you a little gassy, please leave the room to deal with it. You may feel the urge to make a joke and laugh it off, but remember, it may be funny, but it's not very sexy or girly.
- Please don't tell your man when you are constipated or have diarrhea. When in doubt, just place body functions under the TMI category.

- Don't point out pimples, cellulite, wrinkles, or age spots, yours or his. This doesn't change a thing, and chances are, he may not have even noticed, yours or his.
- Please do not talk to him while you are brushing your teeth. Did you ever answer the door for your date with your toothbrush in your mouth? That goes for flossing, too.
- For the women who have had children, make sure he doesn't know about your hemorrhoids.
- If you just got back from the doctor and have a yeast infection, don't share with your man. While I am not suggesting that you keep this information to yourself, you do need to let him know that sex for the moment is not available. Just save him from the gross details.
- If you have a bad cold or flu or are full of snot, keep it to yourself. Does that even sound sexy? And while I am on that subject, please, ladies, I know you would have never blow your nose on a date. Leave the room, take care of your business, and come back.

Ladies, the rule is to not tell your man anything you wouldn't tell him if you were dating and still trying to make an impression. That said, of course, as your level of intimacy and trust is greater, so your discussions will and should reflect the relationship and the life you have built together. My point is that you should remind yourself to maintain the level of appreciation for his feelings and the desire to keep a little mystery between you.

Things Every Woman Should Know

1. Men do not scan a woman's body to see if he can find fat dimples, scars, or unsightly veins. When a man is aroused, he is so caught up in the sexual excitement that lies ahead that he is not combing your body with a fine-tooth comb to see what is imperfect. Men, like wild animals, are too excited

by smells and getting to the main course to even notice your flaws. Remember, if you just stop worrying about them and relax, you will enjoy as much pleasure as he is, I promise you.

2. You should always be ready to try new things. Nothing should be off limits if it gives you and your man pleasure. Men love surprises just as much as we women do. So don't succumb to the same ritual every time you have sex. Keep the spice cabinet filled with new things and the sex cookbook open to try new recipes.

3. Remember, sometimes men don't always know what you want sexually so always ask for what you need. What one woman wants is not always what every woman wants. Don't ever be embarrassed either. Men love it when they are told what to do in bed.

4. Things change over the length of a relationship, and most importantly, our bodies and our thoughts change. So let your partner know if you don't want the same things in the bedroom that you used to want. Maybe he has changed, too, so talk. Don't settle. I have heard that we seem to want something different in clothes, furniture, and so forth every ten years. So, I'm guessing we also have mind changes on sex and how we like it. I heard Jane Fonda on "Good Morning America" (August 8, 2011) promoting her new book *Prime Time,* say, "When women get older and our bodies change, some of us don't want sex at all. Just the intimate loving relationship, and that is okay." Some will explore more sexual ideas because they are more apt to know what they want and aren't afraid to say it.

5. You should stop worrying about how long it is taking you to get aroused. Sometimes we want sex, but when we get started, things enter our minds, and before we know it, we are worried about what we are going to cook for dinner. Then we punish ourselves and our husbands because we

then wonder what the heck is wrong with us. Our minds are very complex and tend to wander off sometimes. Just relax and enjoy what is happening now. Feel your body, and enjoy it.

6. You shouldn't wait too long in between sexual encounters. Some women let life keep them from finding time for sex. If you go too long a period without sex, your body will get used to the abstinence, and pretty soon, your mind will, too. Always find the time.

7. You should find places to have sex other than your bed. Remember, sex is healthy no matter where you do it, like inside, outside, or on the stairs of a vacant building. The out of the norm will give you much more excitement.

8. You should make a date day if you cannot find time for a date night. Make an appointment for sex. Sometimes the plan ahead is more fun because of the expectation. If you have to, really get creative. Make a fake doctor appointment, and get your husband to do the same. It will be the most exciting exam ever.

9. We all wonder if our sex lives are normal and if we are having as much as our neighbor. There is no amount of times per week or month that is normal. As long as you are sexually satisfied and your partner is, then it is normal.

10. Oral sex is a sure way to have an orgasm for most women. Men especially love to give pleasure orally to a woman. Don't let any hang-ups keep you from enjoying something he enjoys doing. Don't forget to splash on a little perfume.

11. You should take time to unwind. Sit and relax with a glass of wine or your favorite beverage. Women seem to always be doing something for someone (work, children, chores, and so forth). You have to take at least fifteen to twenty minutes for yourself to unwind. (I love to enjoy a glass of wine.) Sit in a bath, and listen to music by candlelight. You are worth

the time, and you'll be a happier, healthier person for it. Your husband won't mind the wait.

12. Remember, we women love to be wined and dined. We love romance before sex. For the most part, men are so opposite. They need sex to get into those romantic feelings. So train your man. Remember the book, *Men Are from Mars, Women Are from Venus*? I will write a little synopsis. Once upon a time, Martians and Venusians met, fell in love, and had happy relationships together because they respected and accepted their differences. Then they came to Earth, and amnesia set in. They forgot they were from different planets.

13. All vaginas look different. If you don't like the way yours looks and shy away from letting your man see it in the daylight, relax. There is not one perfect-looking vagina. It's perfect to the one who loves you, so relax and open up. Remember my customer who loved those crotchless panties?

14. Sex on all fours can be a real turn-on. Some women feel a little trampy in that position, but trampy can be fun. Oh, the next time you're in that position, reach through your legs, and take hold of his testicles. Softly stroke them because they are very sensitive, and being too rough is a real turnoff for a man. This can also be the perfect time to hold your vibe against your clitoris for more stimulation, or you can let him hold it there for you.

15. A great kiss can lead to great sex. Make sure you use your tongue, and start off very slowly. Touch him everywhere, and take your time. A long, passionate kiss can take you to a climax quick. As we grow older or are in a long relationship, we tend to peck each other. Pecking should be for chickens only. We need to remember that kissing is usually the first step we take in a relationship. Remember when you were a younger child and you thought one of the girls liked the boy? You would sing the song, "Karen and Bobby, sitting in a tree, k-i-s-s-i-n-g!" So don't stop kissing!

Foreplay and Afterglow

You already know that foreplay is important for women. Sometimes it's the only way we can get in the mood. Today, we'll examine the other side of the sex act, afterplay, or, to borrow a beautiful euphemism, "afterglow." No matter what you call it, they are those warm and quiet moments of satisfaction and completion, and they are just as important.

Cuddle. Spoon. Hold. Have pillow talk. Whatever physical shape your afterglow takes, use it to reignite the closeness that first brought you together. You've just done the most intimate thing imaginable with your man. Now, rest and savor the intimacy that lingers around you both. You can communicate many wonderful and enduring things during this time to deepen this intimacy. If you usually jump up too quickly clean up, don't. Relax and just take a few moments to reflect. Maybe you could whisper in his ear that you wish you could stay in this moment forever. Men love to hear romantic things just like we women do. Sometimes we think things and let them go. We say to ourselves compliments about our man in our thoughts, but we should try saying things aloud. So start talking. Make him feel special.

"What sorts of things should I say?" you ask.

Before I answer that, let me clue you in on some things you probably should not talk about.

- Do not speak of the pressures of work, the worries, and anything that has to do with the children, the mound of unpaid bills overflowing in a basket in the kitchen, or his forgetfulness in taking out the garbage again. In short, stay positive about the sex you just had and about him as a person and a man. Use a tender voice and soft whispers so he can hear the affection you feel for him. Really hold him and rub his chest or squeeze his hand.
- Tell him the things he did right in bed, either generally or specifically. Compliment him on his bedroom skill and

creativity. What are his areas of expertise? Is he a generous lover? You certainly want to vocalize your appreciation for that. Say, "You're so generous in bed. I love that. It's so rare in a man."

- Recognize if he is adept at a particular sexual move. Tell him, "Nobody does that like you." Or remind him that the way he makes love to you is one of the main reasons you fell in love with him because he takes his time and knows how to please you.

- Along the same lines, communicate to him how sexy you still find him. Like women, men longingly remember their younger days, when they were confident with vibrant, studlike manhood. His confidence, like yours, has probably waned over time. Thus, he needs his ego stroked a bit on occasion. You definitely want him to hear that from your mouth, don't you?

A customer, Mrs. X, once told me that she married a very wealthy man who was not that great in bed. Still, every time she told him he was, he showered her with gifts. She said, "Why not tell him how wonderful and fantastic he was?" She made him feel good, and he certainly rewarded her. He always reminded me of Hugh Hefner. When they shopped with me, he just let her choose whatever she wanted and would hand over his credit card to her.

Kind reassurances about his manliness and sex appeal go a long way. The only things that keep some men faithful may be the fact that they can't do better. But why take a chance?

However, just because you're in bed, don't limit your positive afterglow utterances to sex. Don't compliment him merely as a lover, but as a man. Tell him how much you love and appreciate him as a husband, a provider, and a friend. Men are like little boys who swell with pride every time their mother says, "What a good boy you are."

Believe me, all these constructive words and honest compliments merge and make a home in his thoughts more than anything else you can say. He'll love you all the more for them, thus keeping the other woman ("the trollop") at bay.

Now for a little warning . . . To drive home just how important it is to express positive things to your man, we must return to therefore-mentioned Mrs. X. Her story, I fear, takes a disturbing turn. She was the other woman in someone's life.

"It was so easy to take him," she said. "I just gave him lots of compliments and other things he was not getting at home."

So remember, just a few words from your mouth can go a long way to any man. By no means do I approve of her actions. Her behavior was abominable. I only want to remind you and to illustrate a point so you can head off trouble before it starts.

If You Think Your Man Is Cheating

For those of you who have tried everything you know to try, your partner is unwilling to work on the relationship equally, and all your attempts to reignite the romance has failed, then I say, "Life is too short, and you need to move on. First start with moving him out! And most importantly, if you even have an inkling that your man is cheating, there is a good chance he is."

So here are some tips on how to catch your man. Always go with your gut feeling. There are, however, ways to check on your man. You could go out and hire a private eye, or you could get a friend to drive behind him and watch where he goes during the day. There are also tracking devices that you can purchase that attaches to the car and acts like a spy for you.

The following are some known facts a customer related to me. She had just left her attorney and filed for divorce because she caught her husband cheating. She told me she had suspected him because he was getting less and less sexual with her (first big sign) so she started feeling that something was just not right with her man. He was always late coming home and blaming it on work-related meetings. He seemed to be on his cell phone more on the weekends. She told me he started arriving home later and later and had to go out of town more. Her husband started coloring his hair, shaving his testicles, and keeping a toothbrush in his car. Cologne, too! He also started arguments and would then leave the house mad, being gone for hours.

She told me her suspicions were right because she was hanging up his sport coat one night and found several receipts. She confronted him. He said he had to take his client out to entertain him. She asked him point blank if he were cheating.

His answer was, with tears in his eyes, "Babe, I would never cheat on you. I love you, and I am very happy."

She could not understand how he could look her in the eye and lie like that. She almost believed him and then remembered the receipts she had found. You see, the club was an adult massage parlor. She checked it all out and even found out the girl's name.

I just felt so bad for her that I just hugged her. I told her how many times I had heard stories like hers. The conclusion I came up with is that love has absolutely nothing to do with it. Men just cheat for the game and excitement of doing something they know they should not be doing. Some men just cheat because they are stupid and don't think they will get caught, like President Clinton and Tiger Woods. And the list goes on!

Now, while I don't think all men are lying, cheating bastards and have no conscience, I do believe that most men will cheat if they are bored at home and have the freedom and means to have an affair. They don't think about tomorrow. They just let their other head think for them. As a perfect example, John Edwards lost his chance to become president of the United States because he let his penis do his thinking for him.

If you do think your man is cheating, there are websites that can help you and give you some support. I will list the few that have been given to me:

www.catchacheat.com
www.catchspousecheating.com
www.my-cheating-spouse.com
www.surviveanaffair.com
www.staying.com.

My customer also told me to pass this along to any woman who thought her man was cheating:

- Go through his car after he has gone to sleep, especially the trunk.
- Go through the trash, especially if he has one in his bathroom or office.
- Check his mobile phone records and, if you can, his phone for the last number he might have called just before the time he usually walks in the door. Check his incoming last call, especially if it is one past his work hours.
- Check for new clothes. My customer's husband also started buying new clothes, especially new underwear. (That is when she really felt he was cheating.) Before then, she had usually did the clothes buying. How often does your man go buy himself new undies? Well, if he starts, you better not waste any time checking on him.
- Check his computer activities, especially social networking sites.

I had a psychologist in the shop once, and we started talking about life. One thing led to another, and we started talking about men and computers. She told me that the computer is the devil in disguise for marriages. She said that, since the computer has arrived on Earth, her business has skyrocketed. It has made it very easy for men to find all sorts of ways to cheat. So if you suspect your man cheating, check out his computer. You can check the sites he has been on by opening the history button. If you don't know what that is, it is located on the top of your computer, usually beside the favorites button. You can also check his e-mails. Don't forget the sent ones as well as the deleted ones. His mobile phone bill will also be a good place to check.

In ending, I just want to say that, if you have ever been cheated on, there is hope . . . if you still want the relationship to work. I encourage you to get some professional help, with or without him.

Don't do anything else for at least six months. The time will help with the anger you have at wanting to hire a hit man to knock him off the face of the Earth. Even though you feel your life is over and you wish him dead or that a car would run him over, stand back, put the knife back in the drawer, and take a deep breath or maybe two. Take a look at the whole picture, the history you both have. Now take a look at the real meaning of the phrase "the end." Is that really what you want? Remember, the grass is not always greener on the other side of the yard. If you leave your man and find another, chances are, he too comes with some extra baggage.

Sometimes I wonder if staying in my first marriage would have made a difference in my children's lives now that they are adults, so keep that in mind when you are considering not trying to do all you can do to make it work. I know personally that I have guilt within me and will until the day I die. I will always wonder if I have done enough for my children. But then I have to stop and think. Maybe things could have been different, but then again, being different might not have been for the best.

Some women are born to be romantic, like the definition of "the goddess of love." Some are born tomboys in every sense of the word. Then there are the seductive, tantalizing ladies who make men lose their judgment, risk their careers, forget their families, or even fight wars over them. So I will say in respect to all the women who have been cheated on by the other woman, "Karma is a bitch!"

I would like to add one more thing in closing. This bit of advice was given to me years ago, and it helped me a lot, and I hope it will help you. If you do catch your husband or partner cheating, don't hate or blame yourself. Learn to grieve. Give yourself the time it takes to mourn like when you have a death in the family because the pain is just as unbearable. As they say, it takes time to work your way through it. Surround yourself with good friends, and remember, just because he doesn't love you anymore does not mean that no one loves you. I also believe that just because a man has cheated on you does not always make him a cheater. Sometimes a very bad mistake can turn into a well-learned lesson. I think sometimes you need to listen to your heart before you tell him good-bye.

There will likely be times in your life when your soul evolves more quickly than your circumstances. Your subconscious mind may be ready to move forward long before you recognize that you are destined to embrace a new way of life. Your soul intuitively understands that changing habitats can be a vital part of the growth process and there may be one part of you that is eager to move to another home, another state, or another plane of existence. But the ties that bind you to your current mode of being can make moving into this next stage of your life more challenging than it has to be. If you find it difficult to move on, consider that, just as people in your life may come and go, your role in others' lives may also be temporary. And many of the conditions that at first seemed favorable served you for a short time. When you are ready to match your situation to your soul, you will find that you feel a new sense of harmony and increasingly connected to the ebb and flow of the universe.

Epilogue
Last But Not Least

If you feel that this book gears toward bowing down to our man, I guess it does in a way. But isn't that how you got him in the first place? It is our wifely duty. Call me old-fashioned, but we should. It makes us sexy, smart, and mysterious, all the reasons our man chose us out of all the girls out there and any of the ones he dated but did not ask to marry. Go back and read the book, and hopefully you will agree. Isn't your marriage worth it? This comes from sixty years of living and listening to a lot of customers, men and women both, and their trials and tribulations for the past thirty years.

Believe me. Being sixty myself, I know how you feel when insecurities consume your entire body. I felt that lots in my lifetime or when the green-eyed monster paid me a visit on many occasions. I hated the pain that jealousy brought me. So I can honestly tell you that there is nothing that feels more satisfying than when you are enjoying the feeling of sexy. Trust me. It's like a mind game we all have with ourselves. All I am hoping is that something I have said in this book will help you believe that you can be sexy, no matter what age you are.

Once a long time ago, I read a poem about the Secrets of the Mysterious Woman. I can't remember who wrote it or even the entire poem. There was just a few lines that have stuck in my head that I always found very intriguing.

She has a seductive power

It captivates men and can infuriate other women

What makes her so compelling?

Think about it. Maybe what makes the woman in the poem so interesting is all the things she doesn't say!

If you want to captivate your man, learn to be mysterious. Men find a mysterious woman alluring. There is something very exciting and seductive about mysterious women that keeps a man attracted to them. Most men are complicated yet very simple creatures!

Quotes and Quips

- "There is no cosmetic for beauty like happiness." Countess of Blessington
- "Beauty is power; a smile is its sword." Charles Reade
- "In every man's heart there is a secret nerve that answers to the vibrations of beauty." Christopher Morley
- "Beauty when most unclothed is clothed best." Phineas Fletcher
- "If a women rebels against high-heeled shoes, she should take care to do it in a very smart hat." George Bernard Shaw
- "What we obtain too cheaply, we esteem too lightly." Thomas Paine
- "A kiss is a lovely trick designed by nature to stop speech when words become superfluous." Ingrid Bergman
- "A kiss can be a comma, a question mark, or an exclamation point." Mistinguette
- "Laughter is the sun that drives winter from the human face." Victor Hugo
- "The way to love anything is to realize that it might be lost." Gilbert K. Chesterton
- "Love is a canvass furnished by nature and embroidered by imagination." Voltaire
- "I love a hand that meets my own with a grasp that causes some sensation." Samuel Osgood

- "Sex is a flame which uncontrolled may scorch; properly guided, it will light the torch of eternity." Joseph Fetterman
- "Some things are better than sex, and some are worse, but there's nothing exactly like it." WC Fields
- "The most delightful pleasures cloy without variety." Publilius Syrus
- "Sameness is the mother of disgust, variety the cure." Petrarch
- "Being a woman is a terribly difficult task since it consists principally in dealing with men." Joseph Conrad
- "On one issue, at least, men and women agree; they both distrust women." H. L. Mencken
- "Zest is the secret of all beauty. There is no beauty that is attractive without zest." Christian Dior

About the Author

Karen has always been a romantic. From childhood, the Tampa native has loved going to the ocean, taking long walks on the beach, and sitting in the sand to write poetry and romance novels.

In 1986, she opened her first lingerie boutique at the prestigious Reynolda Village, a quaint little shopping village on the grounds of Wake Forest University in Winston-Salem, North Carolina. Taken with a desire to travel, she became a flight attendant with Piedmont/ US Airways and then returned to her first career love, bringing feminine fashions and accessories to women of all ages.

Karen now lives in Charlotte, North Carolina, where she and her husband Bobby own and operate Karen's Beautiful Things, a unique boutique filled with a stunning mixture of charming antiques, eclectic home furnishings, romantic fashions, and alluring lingerie. The two love to travel around the country seeking one-of-a-kind treasures.

Karen has two grown children: Kimberly, a sought-after makeup artist, and Brian, a visual fashion merchandiser manager and freelance interior designer.

Karen's greatest joy is to see that every woman who visits her store has an enjoyable experience shopping and leaves feeling more confident, beautiful, and sexy. This personal concern and interest in others, along with practical advice in the area of romantic relationships, has forged lasting and intimate friendships.

Her collective experience, both personal and vicarious, combined with her instinct for all things romantic and sensuous, is what prompted Karen to write *Be the Other Woman in Your Man's Life*. All stories and anecdotes within its pages originate with real customers. The names have been changed to protect the innocent (and not-so innocent).